SNAPDRAGON

OSPREY
PUBLISHING

SNAPDRAGON

The World War II Exploits of Darby's Ranger and Combat Photographer Phil Stern

PHIL STERN AND LIESL BRADNER

OSPREY
Bloomsbury Publishing Plc
PO Box 883, Oxford, OX1 9PL, UK
1385 Broadway, 5th Floor, New York, NY 10018, USA
E-mail: info@ospreypublishing.com
www.ospreypublishing.com

OSPREY is a trademark of Osprey Publishing Ltd

First published in Great Britain in 2018

A catalogue record for this book is available from the British Library.

ISBN: HB 978 1 4728 2850 7; eBook 978 1 4728 2851 4; ePDF 978 1 4728 2852 1; XML 978 1 4728 2853 8

18 19 20 21 22   10 9 8 7 6 5 4 3 2 1

Index by Zoe Ross
Originated by PDQ Digital Media Solutions, Bungay, UK
Printed in China at C & C Offset Ltd.

Front cover and title page: From a strategic vantage point above the port town of Arzew, Ranger Corporals Robert Bevan and Earl Drost engaged snipers barricaded in warehouses along the waterfront. (Phil Stern)

Osprey Publishing supports the Woodland Trust, the UK's leading woodland conservation charity. Between 2014 and 2018 our donations are being spent on their Centenary Woods project in the UK.

To find out more about our authors and books visit **www.ospreypublishing.com**. Here you will find extracts, author interviews, details of forthcoming events and the option to sign up for our newsletter.

CONTENTS

DEDICATION

For Greg, Mia and Sonny for their constant support. Thanks to the Stern family, David Fahey and staff at Fahey/Klein Gallery, the descendants of World War II Rangers, and my editor Kate Moore whose shared vision made this book possible.

To Phil, thank you for leaving me those little gems along the way that filled in the missing links to your story.

PHIL STERN
1919–2014
In war and in peace, he always remained a Ranger at heart.

NO.. I DON'T KNOW WHAT SHE WAS THINKING —

1953 AT L.A. HOSPITAL BENEFIT.

Phil Stern

PREFACE

On November 14, 2014, I received a voice mail from my dear friend Phil Stern. He was on a rant. The former Ranger was still cursing Old Blood and Guts, 70 years after General Patton's death. The 95-year-old snapper had been reading *Killing Patton*, and wanted to discuss some discrepancies. "Liesl, call me. This guy O'Reilly doesn't know what the hell he's talking about!" he fumed. Stern should know. As a member of Darby's Rangers, the elite Army unit, the World War II vet had a few run-ins with the colorful general in North Africa and Sicily. "The S.O.B. got me on the rear lines in Tunisia without a helmet, fined me $25 bucks and a night in the military slammer!"

Taking a brief pause, he continued with his tirade: "Patton was a piss poor general filled with braggadocio. He had two pearl handle pistols with naked girls on the handle. I'll never forget his shrill voice that spewed profanities. He took over the best hotels and homes and had big parties. In Casablanca he took over a great mansion owned by a French industrialist on the beach."

Phil proposed writing a book with his version of the events, along with other related topics including the invasion of Sicily. I reminded him about his World War II book we'd recently discussed finishing. "What about your

---

Phil poses with his famous subject, Marilyn Monroe. In his later years he mined his vast archives for prints and gallery shows around the world.
TIM MANITONI

memoir?" I reminded him. "Oh, yes, get that published too."

A few months earlier Phil and his son Peter had asked me to spearhead an exhibit of his classic photos, a donation to adorn the empty white walls of the recently built Veterans Home in West Los Angeles. The show would also be a celebration of Phil's 95th birthday that September.

While digging through his extensive archives in his quaint, cluttered Hollywood bungalow across the street from Paramount Studios, I unearthed his original, unfinished, tattered wartime manuscript, buried deep in the bottom of a box underneath a stash of old newspapers from the 1940s. Ignoring the delicate paper disintegrating in my hands, I breezed through the 76 pages, wishing for more. I immediately scanned the crumbling manuscript, then prodded Phil about his memoir and why he never got it published. After being seriously injured during the invasion of Sicily he was medically discharged and sent back to the U.S. With events still fresh in his mind, he began writing his accounts when Hollywood came calling. His career quickly took off with nonstop magazine assignments and work on movie sets as a still photographer. He soon had a large family to support and his manuscript was set aside, forgotten for decades.

What distinguishes Phil's memoir is that, unlike other war photographers on assignment with various news outlets, Stern was a bona fide member of an elite Army unit, allowing him unrestricted access to the front lines, training and behind the scenes of the daily life and shenanigans of the regular G.I.s.

Because Phil was required to do his share of the fighting, his fellow Rangers and other soldiers felt comfortable around him. He was one of them, which allowed him to capture candid moments, intimacy and familiarity in his photographs.

Phil's writing is of the time (*"It's really swell to have pals who will take time out to show a guy how to field strip a gun"*), expressive, comical, sentimental and brutally honest. The boy from Brooklyn admits early on not knowing one end of a rifle from the other. Stern's catchy 1940s lingo, intimate observations and humor transport us back in time, experiencing the horrors of combat and the brotherhood forged during war. Stern introduces us to the hardscrabble Rangers set against the backdrop of the grey, sodden countryside of Scotland, the desert oases of Morocco and the muddied beaches of Mussolini's Italy.

His own photographs reveal a visual timeline of his inevitable transformation from a fresh-faced, enthusiastic G.I., grinning from ear to ear, riding a donkey and skinny dipping in the Mediterranean, to a hardened veteran who has seen the depravity of war. By the time Phil got to Sicily, he didn't expect to make it out alive.

Phil's time in the Army with the Rangers deeply influenced his photographic style and career for the rest of his life. It also put him in good stead with the alpha males of Hollywood: Bogart, Brando, Wayne and Sinatra. They saw him as a man's man and put more trust in him than other photographers. He was seen as a tough guy. They let him into their inner sanctums, snapping photos of unguarded moments.

"I was never interested in the glamour," Phil once said. "I was interested in the tears and agony behind it."

✳ ✳ ✳

Phil began writing his memoir while recuperating from his wounds in Sicily in late 1943, continuing through the fall of 1944. Soon work and family became his priorities, taking up the majority of his time so the manuscript was put aside and never completed until now.

When Phil passed away on December 13, 2014, I took up the reins in finishing his wartime memoir as per his wishes. In addition to countless interviews and intimate conversations with Phil and his family through the years, I also spoke with relatives of the 1st Battalion Rangers who knew Phil, acquaintances, coworkers and longtime friends he confided in. In addition to Phil's original text, chapters also include quotes from fellow Rangers, reporters and photographers culled from his archives, research, personal interviews and notes.

In order to understand the different voices being expressed by the authors throughout the book we have retained Phil's original memoir in a typewriter style font to closely reflect the era in which it was written.

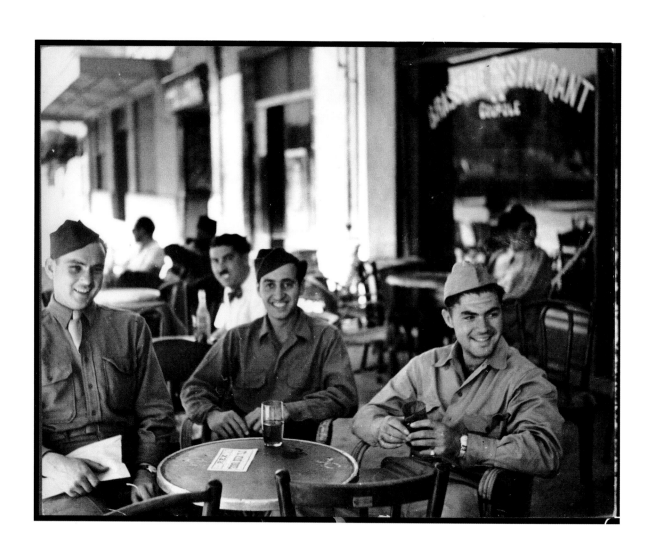

PROLOGUE

DECEMBER 1943, U.S.A.

This is about a guy that gets shot up in the war and gets back to the U.S. on a medical and turns out to be a sort of oddity in his hometown. People fling questions at him. "Howdya feel under fire huh? What's your reaction when the slugs hit ya? Lots of pain?" When these queries are reasonably answered there follows a group of questions not quite so bloodthirsty such as, "What are the Germans like? The Italians? How about the girls in North Africa and Sicily? What about the cities? Tell us some funny experiences you've had," and on and on and on.

So naturally our hero develops a hoarse throat and glib story-telling technique derived purely from the weight and number of questions fired at him. After a few months he wonders whether half the yarns he tells really happened. Also, he starts to get sort of bored with himself and accuses himself of being a long-winded so and so. Of course a guy that's as hammy as me will get a big bang out of being in the center of all such questioning.

This local café was a popular haunt for the Rangers to relax and knock down a couple libations. Located near the middle of the town square in Nemours, Algeria, they could take in the local scenery while dining alfresco.
PHIL STERN ARCHIVES

13

I must confess a growing delight with every new questioner especially when they say, "Gosh, but you've sure been around and we people here at home know so little about the hardships of you boys overseas."

Another problem comes up: getting enough sleep. All of his globetrotting G.I. friends invite him to dinners, parties, gatherings and bars just for the poor guy to relate stories and answer questions. They want to know all the gory details and then some. And this routine has simply gotten me sort of sick, underweight and generally bleary eyed from the lack of sleep. Despite my love and satisfaction of supplying gratification to all my friends' curiosity, I just can't take it anymore. Hence this book. I'll just carry copies around and throw them at people. Maybe now I'll get some sleep.

INTRODUCTION

FROM NEW YORK CITY TO HOLLYWOOD

Growing up on the gritty streets of New York City, the one thing Phil Stern decided early on was that he would never be a salesman, à la Willy Loman, like his father. Born September 3, 1919, in Philadelphia to Russian Jewish emigrants Alexander and Mae, Phil was an infant when his parents and two older brothers packed up and moved to Brooklyn. "During the days of the very acute depression, we moved around the boroughs a lot," he recalled. "We were always two steps ahead of the sheriff in paying the rent."

Phil's lifelong passion for photography began when he was 12 years old. "My mother found an Eastman Kodak advertisement in the newspaper. They were offering any 12-year-old kid a free, brand new Kodak camera. It was one of those box cameras. I was fascinated with the images it made. I thought it was pure magic. Photography became my life."

12-year-old Phil found his calling early on when he got a Kodak Brownie Box camera. Honing his craft as an 18-year-old apprentice in photo labs on Canal Street, he was quickly discovered by editors for the *Police Gazette, Friday* and left-leaning *PM Magazine*. Later sent to Hollywood, he landed his first assignment of many for *Life* magazine.

As a teenager, Phil worked after school in photo labs and art studios sweeping the floors and getting an education in cleaning photographic dark rooms, mixing chemicals and loading film-plates for bulky cameras. "I was an all-around gadabout."

Soon he began working in a cheap, grimy photoengraving shop on Canal Street. At night he took photos of dead bodies for the *Police Gazette* at $3.00 a pop. Phil's career got a big boost in 1939 when 23-year-old millionaire publisher Dan Gillmor strolled into his shop one day and hired Phil on the spot as the staff photographer for his new left-wing magazine, *Friday*. Seated around a huge oval table for his first staff meeting, Phil was dumbfounded when he realized he was in the company of literary and artistic greats Richard O. Boyer, Erskine Caldwell, artist John Groth and photography scholars Eliot Elisofen and Lewis Hines. For his first assignment he would accompany *New Yorker* writer Ruth McKenney to Harlan County, Kentucky, for a feature on the plight of coal miners.

In early 1941, Gillmor sent Phil to California to open their Hollywood office, earning $60 a week. He took jobs on the side as a set photographer, starting at the top with Orson Welles' *Citizen Kane* and *The Magnificent Ambersons*. On set he met Welles' Director of Photography, Gregg Toland, who became his mentor of sorts along with Chinese-American cinematographer James Wong Howe, a master of film noir-esque lighting. The two men shared a belief in the importance of light and shadow, which greatly influenced Phil's shooting style throughout his career.

When *Friday* folded in September 1941, Phil approached magazine editors and was quickly hired, working freelance for *Life, Colliers, Saturday Evening Post, Look, Photoplay* and another recently launched progressive daily titled *PM Magazine*.

On the day that would go down in infamy, December 7, 1941, Phil was on assignment for *Popular Photography*, shooting the San Bernardino, California, unit of the Women's Ambulance and Defense Corps of America (WADCA). Phil recounted the eerie scene that later became the Picture of the Month in June 1942.

Taking this shot was a weird experience for me. It was early Sunday morning, December 7, 1941. This realistic scene with gas masks was enacted for practice purposes. Suddenly the field radios blared out, "The Japs have just bombed Pearl Harbor! The West Coast Army Command orders all Officers and National Guardsmen to report to their post at once!" A very quiet period followed and the drills proceeded in the same manner but a more determined look was draped across everyone's face.

Starlet Rita Hayworth on the cover of the *Police Gazette*. For a brief time Phil worked for the periodical made famous by reporter/photographer Weegee. His job consisted mainly of taking photos of dead bodies and risqué gals.

POLICE GAZETTE

The Women's Ambulance Corps of Hollywood don gas masks in the early morning sun amid a backdrop of smoke from smudge pots. The movie studios supplied the smudge pots, special effects and stretchers. Phil took this shot during the first demonstration under air-raid conditions on December 7, 1941.

PHIL STERN

A reserve officer at Paramount Studios recommended Phil enlist right away. "Look Phil," he said, "You're young and healthy so why don't you volunteer so you can continue photography and we'll make sure you get to do what you love doing, photography, instead of driving some truck." At the time Phil was 21 years old. "I believed I was invincible," he said. "I wanted to go to war to destroy Hitler." He soon found himself on a train bound for Astoria, Long Island, to enter the Army Signal Corps. Because of his prior training as a professional photographer, Phil was given a noncommissioned officer's ranking of staff sergeant. He was shipped off to the Signal Corps Replacement Training Center at Camp Crowder, a military installation near Neosho, Missouri. Soldiers were trained in 40 different military communications specialties involving radio, radar, telegraphy, photography, maintenance and even pigeon wrangling. After a few weeks' paperwork delay, Staff Sergeant Stern was sailing through thousands of miles of U-boat-infested waters in the Atlantic, eventually steaming safely into the United Kingdom.

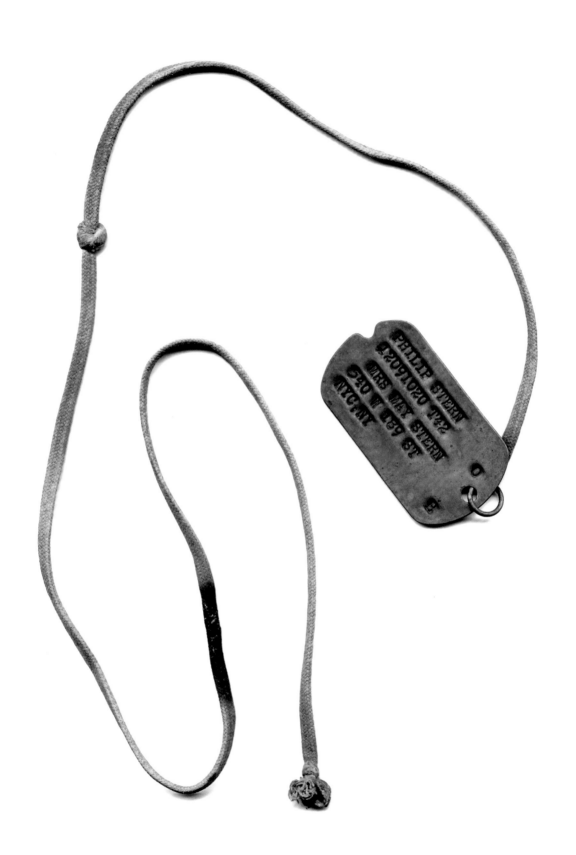

CHAPTER 1

LONDON

YANKS INVADE THE UNITED KINGDOM

By the time the first American troops set foot on the shores of the United Kingdom on January 26, 1942, the Allies had been at war for nearly two and a half years. While the United States had remained neutral at the onset of the war, the Germans were storming across Europe, conquering enemies at lightning bolt speed since first invading Poland in 1939. Japan's bombing of Pearl Harbor on December 7, 1941, hastened America's entry into the war. U.S. forces were immediately deployed to Great Britain, which served as a critical base for American operations throughout the next four years. The 34th "Red Bull" Infantry Division and the 1st Armored Division were the first American contingents to cross the Atlantic, landing in the northern cities of Belfast, Glasgow and Liverpool.

The Eighth Air Force arrived in June and began training at Bushy Park, 15 miles west of London. Phil would join his compatriots in London in the summer of 1942 and eventually some 1.4 million Americans were posted around the United Kingdom, from Scotland to Cornwall, in preparation for D-Day.

"He's in the Army now." With dog tags and a United States Army Signal Corps card, Phil became an official Army photographer. After a short stint at the Signal Corps Replacement Training Center at Camp Crowder in Missouri he was shipped off to London. Now to make good.
PHIL STERN

The War Department provided American G.I.s with a slim, six-page pamphlet: *Instructions for American Servicemen in Britain 1942*. It discussed culture, lingo, history and essential advice such as "Never criticize the King or Queen, their food or coffee."
STEPHEN BARNES / ALAMY STOCK PHOTO

A few months after signing up with the Signal Corps, Phil was shipped overseas to London where he worked in the dark room, taking portraits of stuffy generals and elite social life. Here he takes his chances near an unexploded bomb in Westminster.
U.S. ARMY SIGNAL CORPS

Even if stationed in northern England and Scotland, sooner or later all eager young American servicemen would make their way to London. Young men from small town U.S.A. rarely wandered out of their own neighborhoods, let alone traveled abroad. So walking through the streets of bustling, wartime London was exciting but overwhelming. To help familiarize servicemen with their new surroundings, the War Department provided them with a slim, six-page pamphlet: *Instructions for American Servicemen in Britain, 1942*. It discussed culture, lingo, history and essential advice such as: "Never criticize the King or Queen, their food or coffee." It also clarified how the British were reserved, not unfriendly, and might appear soft-spoken and polite. They were not "panty-waists" (slang for effeminate or weak), noted the manual.

While some boys wrote home about the lack of sunshine and the warm beer, attention lavished on them from zealous English girls soon made up for the grey skies and fog. They heard that Yanks came bearing gifts of chewing gum, nylon stockings and cigarettes, and tossed money around like kings, much to the dismay and resentment of their British comrades. Indeed, the average salaries for American G.I.s were five times what a British Tommy was paid. Brash, clean shaven and smartly dressed in new, modern uniforms, it was no wonder women swooned over the Americans with their movie-star looks. Their British counterparts were poorly kitted out, forced to wear their sack-like battledress and hobnail boots at all times. They'd grumble that American G.I.s were "overpaid, oversexed and over here."

Food rationing, which began in 1940, was a shock for some: however, many American boys had grown up during the Great Depression and were quite familiar with hard work and living on scraps. What they weren't accustomed to was seeing bombed-out homes and air-raid shelters.

The British were grateful and welcomed their Allies with a "Salute the Soldier" week, with parades of American servicemen marching through the streets of London. Local pubs and dance clubs were simply overflowing with Yanks. On the corner of Shaftesbury Avenue and Denman Street, "Rainbow Corner," the American Red Cross Club near Piccadilly Circus, was one of the most popular hangouts. Open 24 hours a day, the club served up all the comforts of home: waffles, hamburgers, doughnuts, coffee and endless Coca-Colas. G.I.s introduced British hostesses to jazz and the jitterbug with music performed by bands with names such as The Flying Forts, The Flying Yanks and the Hepcats.

Phil soaked up the heady atmosphere, but after several weeks in the capital, Staff Sergeant Stern had had his fair share of sightseeing and carousing during his time off from the Signal Corps Photo Lab in northeast London. He was ready for action, something more challenging so he could get on with the war and go home. Enter the Rangers.

***

JULY 29 - SEPTEMBER 23, 1942

Seems like everything started at 35 Davis Street in London. What a city. Just like back in New York. England's Capital has a subway system called the underground which I think is better than the New York tubes. The cars have plush seats, are cleaner, quieter and generally more comfortable even if the cost is a few pennies more. Department stores like Selfridges on Oxford Street correspond to Macy's and Gimbels. There's Hyde Park with its screwball orators who yell at you saying that the reason for war and misery in the world is because people eat meat. Trafalgar Square where the little kids and old guys come along for the day just to feed the pigeons and watch all the people and vehicles go by. And Piccadilly Circus, the amusement area – movies, plays, vaudeville, pubs, stores and throngs of soldiers, sailors, civilians pacing the streets as well as the sidewalks. A New York kid sort of feels at home in a place like this. Anyway, most of the time was spent working. Sightseeing only took place at night and Sundays (can't kick about that). My work consisted of helping out in the Signal Corps photographic dark room and going out on picture taking jobs.

Major Cuthbertson was the boss and one day he sent me to 20 Grosvenor Square, Allied HQ, to make some headshots of a two-star general. I can't mention his name because of military security. Don't remember it anyway. This general turns out to be a very soldierly looking man with gray hair and distinguished and just what I always pictured a general to look like. Of course, Sergeant Stern had just been in uniform about forty or fifty days up to this point and many civilian habits remained intact. Our general was on the real high end of the military ladder and me at the other end. "General," I said. "You have a dead pan expression. Couldn't you loosen up a bit? Perhaps a light conversation with your aide would help?" The General, the Colonel and a few visiting admirals gave me a funny look and the whole bunch began laughing. I shot two flashes and got some pretty good photos. On the way out, a press relations officer cut into me for action so un-G.I. with the high command. He may have been right but the two-star General didn't complain, nor did any of his high-ranking associates. And STARS AND STRIPES ran a highly satisfactory picture of the General. No harm done at all, I figured. Such is the kind of work I get tied up with. When I didn't shoot pictures, there was plenty of dark room work.

Seeing the sights of London was a lot of fun. But where was the war, the excitement, the shellfire, the Nazis and all the combat scenes I joined the Army to photograph? So far, the closest I get to war is the beautiful apartment part of my company is billeted in. You see, we have a scene from the living room window, which shows the adjacent building leveled by a big German bomb. A guy should get the Purple Heart for the feeling he gets after seeing that. I should add that these apartments used to be occupied by wealthy Londoners who left for the suburbs immediately following the blitz. Also, I might say that these

General Eisenhower's chief of staff, Lieutenant General Walter Bedell Smith, was probably the top-secret general that Phil was assigned to photograph at Allied Headquarters in July 1942. Postwar, Smith was an ambassador to the Soviet Union and director of the Central Intelligence Agency.
PHIL STERN

flats had fancy wood work and big mirrors but that was all nullified by strictly G.I. furnishings - army cots, barracks bags, ash trays, cartons of Camels and ESQUIRE gals (wall pictures of course). So my spirits are pretty low until I read in STARS AND STRIPES about the Rangers asking for volunteers. My decision was to become a Ranger by hook or crook. I developed a plan of action and carefully planned a song-and-dance to hand Major Cuthbertson who would be the final say in any transfer I might make.

THE STARS AND STRIPES

Men Wanted For Tough Job

Volunteers Face Rigid Qualifications

Anyone interested in coming to grips with the enemy—personally—has only two days to sign up. But the requirement says you can't be higher in rank than a private first class, unless you're a technician.

In terse notification, the Base Headquarters Commandant let it be known that any enlisted man "desiring to volunteer for hazardous combat duty" should report to the Sergeant Major at Headquarters. The announcement called for the following qualifications:

1—at least five feet six inches in height.

2—normal weight.

3—not over 35 years of age.

4—excellent condition.

5—no record of trial by court-martial.

6—character rating of excellent.

7—not over grade of private first class (unless technician).

8—completed basic infantry training (but need not be infantryman).

9—no applications will be accepted after 1200 May 21.

If you can fill these requirements, and are anxious to get nasty with those Nazis, walk, do not run to Headquarters.

Seeing the sights of London was fun but Phil was anxious to see action and fight the Germans. As fate would have it he spotted a notice in the *Stars and Stripes* newspaper looking for volunteers "anxious to get nasty with those Nazis … in an elite hit-and-run unit" that would send him on a life-changing adventure with the Rangers.

STARS AND STRIPES

A very ironic situation turns out of this. While I'm conniving all this stuff, the Major decides to send a photographer to the Rangers and can't find any volunteers. Seems some high-ups want a photographic record of the First Ranger Battalion. Major Cuth was probably a bit worried about the Ranger detail and since it was a volunteer group no man could merely be ordered to join up. So I walked into Cuthbertson's office completely unaware of his desire to get a man for the Rangers. I was seething a bit and had a hard time getting started.

"Sir," I said, "I would like to join the Rangers. I'm young enough, healthy, I like rough living, have a flair for excitement and besides I have a thorough belief in our war cause and want to help fight for it a little more concretely than by photographing military big shots." I expected to be thrown out on my ear. I hardly believed it but the old Major put his arm around me and says, "Son, how're you feeling lately? Did you get all your rations? Here have some of these Nestles bars" (tough stuff to get, by the way). "So you want to join the Rangers my boy? Of course you realize it's a rough 'n tough outfit. And it's not so easy to get into their group. Of course with a lot of effort and knowing the right people, it might be arranged. Now are you sure you really would like to tie up with Colonel Darby's Rangers?" "Absolutely, Sir," was my reply. My C.C. picks up the phone, makes a call, and within fifteen minutes the paperwork gets started and shortly after Mrs. Stern's little boy officially becomes a "Ranger."

CHAPTER 2

SCOTLAND

THE FORMATION OF THE RANGERS

When the United States finally entered the war after the attack on Pearl Harbor on December 7, 1941, President Roosevelt realized American troops lacked combat experience and were ill equipped to successfully strike back against the battle-hardened Axis powers. In a meeting with military leaders, Major General Dwight D. Eisenhower proposed the establishment of a hit and run unit, similar in formation to the British Commandos who had been racking up victories in raids against the German-held Lofoten Islands in Norway.

The formal origins of the World War II Rangers commenced in the early spring of 1942. General George Marshall, Chief of Staff of the United States Army, visited Great Britain for a meeting with Admiral Lord Louis Mountbatten, the charismatic head of British Combined Operations Headquarters. Impressed by the Commando training center in Scotland, Marshall sent Colonel Lucian K. Truscott, a former cavalry officer in World War I, to England to coordinate the formation of an elite American raiding force to be trained by the battle-proven British Commandos as soon as possible.

A group of fresh-faced Rangers enthusiastically charge through the mud with rifles and guns wearing old-style M1917 helmets from World War I, often referred to as shrapnel helmets or Tommy helmets by the British and doughboy helmets in the United States.
PHIL STERN

Darby shells out orders while American Rangers trudge through the muddied campground past their pyramidal tents. Phil arrived at Corker Hill just as the Rangers were returning from their comfortable accommodations in Dundee, September 1942.
PHIL STERN

European theater commander General Dwight D. Eisenhower impressed upon Truscott that the new unit should be named something other than "Commandos," "for the glamour of that name will always remain and properly so – British."

Truscott chose a name steeped in American military history. The term Ranger harkens back to the early 17th century and the Colonial and Revolutionary war era. The moniker is most commonly associated with Rogers' Rangers, who fought for the British during the French and Indian Wars. Famous American Rangers include Daniel Boone and Abraham Lincoln.

The officer Truscott chose to lead the new battalion was 31-year-old Captain William Orlando Darby, described by Truscott as "outstanding in appearance, possessed of a most attractive personality ... keen, intelligent, and filled with enthusiasm." William "Bill" Darby was born on February 8, 1911 in Fort Smith, Arkansas, a former frontier military post. Upon graduation from the U.S. Military Academy at West Point in 1933, Darby was commissioned as a second lieutenant, assigned to a mounted artillery unit at Fort Bliss, Texas. His exceptional leadership skills and amiable disposition quickly earned him a promotion to captain.

Recruiting immediately began with officers, chosen by Darby, on June 8, and the selection of enlisted volunteers started on June 11. The majority of G.I.s were culled from the first U.S. companies to reach the shores of Northern Ireland: the 34th Division, 1st Armored Division and V Corps. Candidates had to pass the requisite requirements, both physical and mental, to simply get an interview. Naturally athletic individuals with good stamina were what was required. Men ranging in age from 17 to 25 were peppered with a host of questions:

- Do you have the guts to stick a knife in a man's back and twist it?
- Are you a good swimmer?
- Describe how you would assault a machine gun position if you were leading a 12-man squad landing on an enemy-held beach.
- How would you destroy a train without explosives if you were trapped behind enemy lines?

Of the approximately 2,000 men who applied, 500 were selected. Officially activated on June 19, 1942, in Carrickfergus, Northern Ireland, the 1st Ranger Battalion was initially formed with the purpose of carrying out raids against the enemy. Darby's Rangers would be trained to hit and run under the cover of darkness, land on enemy beaches and storm gun positions.

On June 28, 1942, the Rangers began exercises at the British Commando Training Depot at Achnacarry in Scotland. The tiny, quaint hamlet consisted mainly of an estate and castle, the ancestral home of the Chiefs of Clan Cameron located in Lochaber, a mountainous region in the Highlands of Scotland. The Commando-style training would be overseen by Lieutenant Colonel Charles Vaughan. In his memoir, Darby described the burly, six foot two, 50-year-old World War I veteran as "remarkably agile with a face which showed storm clouds and at other times, warm sunniness."

For the next three months, the Rangers hopscotched across northern Scotland from Achnacarry and the remote, midge infested Glen Crippesdale island, and on to the more civilized Dundee, then completing their formal training in the dreary, muddy fields of Corker Hill, southwest of Glasgow.

Reveille by bagpipe, which the Rangers hated worse than bugles, announced the start of their day. The Brits would constantly taunt the Rangers with what

ABOVE Rangers arriving from Dundee head to their temporary homes in Corker Hill. The bivouac area had rows of pyramidal tents that fitted up to six soldiers. An Intelligence officer dumped Phil into one of the tents and told him to make friends with an eccentric cast of men. In the foreground a Ranger carries his guitar through the mud-filled paths.

PHIL STERN

LEFT Fully loaded Ranger in Achnacarry, Scotland, 1942. Along with the usual infantry equipment, Rangers had to pack special equipment during training such as a collapsible rubber dinghy and life vest for amphibious landings. They also carried demolition gear and camouflage nets. This clever Ranger somehow made space for his can of Planters peanuts.

PHIL STERN

Everyone was required to know their weapons before using them. They were trained to operate all company weapons and many of the enemy's. The Rangers had a fondness for mortars, fired with uncanny accuracy developed by regular practice. Pictured is Sergeant James B. Hanson handling a Tommy gun. Missing is the Bazooka rocket launcher, another heavily used Ranger weapon.

PHIL STERN

LEFT Settling in at Corker Hill, Phil met with Darby to get the skinny on his precise function. Life with the 1st Ranger Battalion was the real deal for the wide-eyed Stern, who had skipped basic training with the Signal Corps. Darby would accept him as official photographer, but with the caveat that he was required to pass the rigorous training set forth for all Rangers. This consisted of speed marches, cliff climbing, bayonet training and the famous "death slide" obstacle course.

PHIL STERN

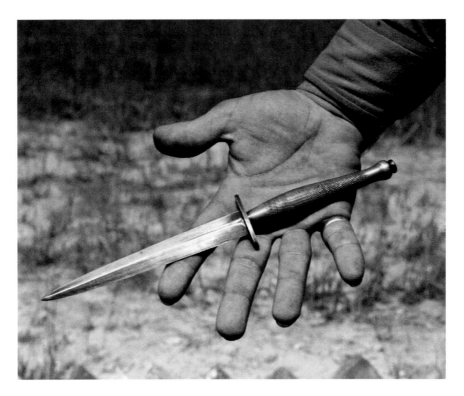

now seem like rather tame verbal heckles: "You lousy Americans! Ice cream guzzlers! You Coca-Cola hounds!"

Three main tenets of their training focused on physical fitness, weaponry and small unit tactics. Rangers were subjected to some of the most grueling training shelled out during World War II. There were 20-mile speed marches, cliff climbing, bayonet and barbed wire obstacle courses, a death slide across a raging river and instruction in the art of guerilla warfare, from hand-to-hand fighting to demolitions and night fighting. Later they would be subjected to amphibious training with live ammunition and grenades.

Phil arrived at Corker Hill on September 24, 1942, just as the Rangers were returning from three weeks of coastal raiding training in Dundee. There, they were billeted with locals in comfortable accommodations, treated to home cooked meals and enjoyed the company of many a young lass. The initiation of Darby's buddy system along with exhaustive training had created strong bonds between the men. It didn't take long for Phil to fit in.

✳✳✳

SEPTEMBER 24, 1942. CORKER HILL, SCOTLAND

I knew I was going into a fighting outfit so I sold everything I owned and spent as much money as I could. I didn't want to have anything to go back to. If I had something to go back to, I might be too careful and try to value my life above everything else. My new outfit is supposed to be in a little town of Salen in Scotland. My travel orders read that way. The London Midlands Scotland railway gets me for a customer. We choo-choo our way up to Scotland. By we, I meant Lieutenant Freddie Fox and myself.

LEFT TOP The British Commando Fairbairn–Sykes Knife was issued to the 1st Ranger Battalion at Achnacarry. The double-edged dagger was developed by William Fairbairn and Eric Sykes while serving with the Shanghai Municipal Police. Associated with World War II elite forces, it had a slender blade that could easily penetrate a ribcage, and was designed for surprise attacks and hand-to-hand fighting.
PHIL STERN

LEFT Log Drills: Physical training with logs developed lean and strong physiques necessary for the vigorous challenges that lay ahead. In the front of the line is six-foot tall Warren "Bing" Evans, a former football player from University of Minnesota, a prime example of physical fitness.
PHIL STERN

Speed March: Beginning with a 30-mile jaunt at a rapid stride, a company of Rangers step briskly during a speed march through the picturesque Scottish countryside. Five miles an hour was a daily grind for these stalwarts, who claimed the speed march as a secret weapon.
PHIL STERN

Fox was responsible for my reaching my destination and outfit. And the good Lieutenant sure had plenty navigating problems. The Rangers had left Dundee while we were en route but Lieutenant Fox was undaunted and by proper inquiries he figured out the new Ranger headquarters. So we end up at Corker Hill, a mud-flat right outside of Glasgow. Fox officially delivers me, gets his receipt, and happily prances back to London.

Well, here I am with the First Ranger Battalion. They have a real bivouac area with rows and rows of tents with real soldiers dotting up the area. They even carry guns; big ones, little ones, short ones, long ones. They are rough looking guys and so was the language they used. Frankly, I'm a bit scared. I don't even know one end of a rifle from the other. I just about understand that the bullet simply must come out the end where I can see a long dark hole. You see I never had basic training. The Army sent me over as a photographic specialist. These guys were plenty busy and the Ranger intelligence officer dumps me into one of those six men pyramidal tents and tells me to make friends with the boys until tomorrow when I'm to meet the Colonel and get myself generally oriented. So I start to make friends. And boy, are these guys interesting. I'll give you a cross section of the kind of fellows that become Rangers and why. Johnny, a Greek lad, says he got married while he was on the Louisiana maneuvers. A swell gal but he neglected to relate this matter to the girl he married in Los Angeles. This L.A. gal finds out and makes an issue out of the thing. The Louisiana dame gets wind of the California gal and raises hell. Johnny is saved by sudden overseas shipment. He now feels a lot more comfy in a rough fighting outfit than being back home to face that wife problem. Oh yeah, Johnny used to run a gin mill back in Ohio.

Walt just got out of school before he got into the army. He always had a weird curiosity about how it would feel to kill a guy. "But," says Walt, "They put you in the jug and electrocute you for killing a guy back in the States. But here," announces our boy with a gleam in his eye, "it's legal." He adds (and this will kill you), "I've learned how to kill a guy in about three seconds without him making a sound. So what I want to do is to sneak up on a German barracks at night and put about twenty or thirty of the Nazis into a permanent sleep." A Jewish boy, Murray Ketzen from Brooklyn, says he's fed up with hearing some guys rave that Jews are yellow and are scared to join combat outfits. And that all they want to do is join quartermaster depots and medical units. So Murray wallops an anti-Semite on the head with an Irish beer bottle and then puts in his application to join the Rangers. He made it.

Jim claims he used to tame lions for Frank Buck.* His life has been one of constant thrills and excitement. He's sort of geared for that kind of living and feels that the Ranger Battalion is quite compatible with his personality.

Here's the payoff: One guy, Mike, tells me, "Look Phil, I haven't been too good a boy in my time. I palled around with the

---

*   Frank Buck was a famous American hunter and animal collector, also known for the books and movies based on his exploits.

A Commando instructor follows a 1st Battalion Ranger as they leap from a 20-foot-high wooden structure into a mud hole, one of three obstacles on the Tarzan Course at the Commando training depot in Scotland.
PHIL STERN / U.S. ARMY SIGNAL CORPS

TOP Obstacle Course: General Truscott, Major Darby and Commando instructors look on as members of the 1st Battalion vent their fury on hapless dummies at the end of the rigorous "bullets and bayonet" obstacle course. The Rangers broke Commando records for this course. Consisting of simple wooden structures and complicated, miles-long trails with mud pits and barbed wire, it was at the center of the training regimen.
PHIL STERN

ABOVE Swimming in an icy stream with full equipment and raging water was part of the Commando training Rangers had to master before they could qualify. Those who failed were returned to their former units.
PHIL STERN

From left to right: James Altieri, Peer Buck and Randall Harris.
PHIL STERN

wrong crowd and ended up in lots of trouble. Yep, I'm wanted in four states for robbery, extortion and forgery. The FBI and state cops are after my ass. I'm safer here with the Rangers and what's more, this is my chance to make good. I ain't kicking." Then we have Peer Buck who was a hotel dick in Minneapolis. Well, you can't blame Peer for tying up with the Rangers. Anything would be better than being a hotel dick in Minneapolis. And of course the general run of kids in this volunteer group are just healthy guys out to do a necessary job and get some real excitement in the process. I feel that way myself.

I forgot to mention my very good friend in the transportation section of the First Ranger Battalion. He's a big strong guy and it's not fiction to say that he can easily lift a jeep anytime he feels like it. He's a full-blooded Sioux Indian and owns many acres of farmland in South Dakota. His vocabulary is very limited. I consider myself a pal of his and yet in the one year time of our acquaintance, I've only heard him say about 12 words and about half a dozen grunts. His name is Sampson P. Oneskunk and I never

ABOVE LEFT Toggle Bridge: Rangers attempt a precarious crossing on a toggle bridge over a swiftly moving river. This required the use of toggle ropes, each about four feet in length, with a piece of wood at one end and a loop at the other. When linked together they had a variety of uses.

PHIL STERN, SOURCED FROM LT. W T LOCKEYEAR / IWM / GETTY

ABOVE RIGHT Mountaineering: Medical officer Captain "Doc" Jarrett descends a 300-foot cliff from a mountaintop. Rope techniques were practiced while scaling down an old ivy-covered Scottish castle. While scaling the Arbroath cliff in Dundee, a falling boulder knocked Ranger Simon Gomez 100 feet to the ground.

PHIL STERN

could find out what his middle initial represented. Anyway, old Sam is a friend to everybody and he never fails to pitch in whenever there is a tough detail to handle. Naturally, I'm greatly impressed with my new group of friends and could hardly sleep all night. I just kept thinking and wondering about the experiences ahead. I worried a bit about how the folks back home would feel about me getting into a roughhouse bunch like the Rangers. Secretly though, I felt quite impressed with myself. Boy, what will those subway commandos back in New York think now. They'll be jealous as hell. Well, I'm sitting on top of the world. Of course I have no right to think along such lines. I still can't even fire a gun.

ABOVE Ranger patch: To boast morale, a battalion-wide contest was organized to see who could design the best Ranger patch. Sergeant Anthony Rada from Flint, Michigan, won with his red, white and blue scroll patch that resembled the British Commando insignia.
PHIL STERN

LEFT Private First Class Roland Retting from Minnesota sews the new Ranger emblem on Sergeant Rada. Later the Rangers had to remove anything identifying them, due to Axis Sally's warning on the radio that "Every Ranger captured will be killed by his own knife," after the knife and bayonet bloodbath at Sened Station.
NATIONAL ARCHIVES

No training. Gads, I might even catch pneumonia in this foggy cold weather and boy does it get foggy in Scotland. So I start counting 30-caliber bullets and fall asleep.

Some corporal sounds off reveille at 6 a.m. I'm up and ready for anything. Didn't even want to continue sleeping. Waded through eight inches of mud for some powdered egg and bacon. It tasted wonderful even though the other guys made faces at the stuff and expressed their feelings in very impolite language. I believe my enthusiasm that morning wasn't much appreciated by the Rangers. Well, now to see what's cooking with the Ranger high command and what their attitude toward me is. My first meeting is with Captain Bill Martin, a tall, lanky intelligence officer from Minneapolis where he was a private detective. Martin comes out of an old artillery outfit and sure knows his big guns. The captain is very friendly and a big smile runs all across his puss. "Good to meet you Stern," he says. "See the supply sergeant and draw your side arms and other necessary equipment. The old man is tied up but would like to see you." Martin runs off to a large tent where a lot of guys are milling around. Curious, I follow. "What's the deal?" I ask one of the men. "By God," he says, "we're finally getting our First Ranger shoulder patches. We've been waiting weeks." It looked like a bunch of kids lined up for free ice cream. A wooden bench inside the tent contained

a platter full of the new Ranger insignias and Captain Martin was distributing them to the men who paid in advance and made orders. Standing around the table, beaming and proud, was Corporal Tony Rada* who designed the shoulder patch and received a 25 buck bonus for it from the First Ranger Battalion commanding officer, Colonel Darby. Tony had good reason to be proud. He lived and worked in Flint, Michigan, in the automobile factories. He also took up artwork and had been looking for a chance to use his talents within the Army. This was his opportunity and Tony made good. Over five hundred men's shoulders prove it. I like Tony a lot and we became friends fast. I get to know Tony's pal Denny Bergstrom very well and in the evening all three of us got passes and headed for Glasgow which is just a twenty minute bus ride away. And the fare is only a penny. We're all in pretty good spirits although I'm anxious to meet Colonel Darby and learn about my exact function in my new job with his "lads."

The evening in Glasgow was indeed an interesting one. We ran the gamut. We ate a chicken dinner, walked into a pub and get drunk on black beer. We get into a street fight with some of the guys from the 18th Infantry then sauntered up to the Locarno Dance Hall and cavorted with some nice looking gals from the neighborhood. We're all a bit woozy and can't quite make out officers from enlisted men. And more than three second looies are called names other than they were conditioned for at O.C.S. Officer Candidate School. A few more scuffles in the dark and back to Corker Hill we stagger. For the first time I feel like a real soldier.

* * *

It was during Phil's initiation into the Ranger battalion that he earned the nickname "Snapdragon." Ranger James Altieri recounts the episode in his memoir, *The Spearheaders*, published in 1960:

---

*   Most histories of the Rangers have Rada's rank as a sergeant as opposed to corporal as Phil remembered him.

It happened one day as the Rangers were returning to camp from a grueling speed march, led by the thundering, self-assured First Sergeant Donald Torbett. Phil suddenly appeared, loaded down with several cameras and a pack full of film. A moonfaced stocky sergeant, Phil was a strange-looking apparition that seemed to burst with excitement as he ran alongside us, puffing heavily and snapping pictures. He immediately zoomed in on First Sergeant Donald Torbett, who at the time was belaboring the Rangers to "get their asses off the ground. You're moving like a bunch of WACS!" (Women's Air Corps). Phil shouted out to Torbett, "That was great! Would you do that again, please? That'd make a good layout of a tough Ranger sergeant for the Stars and Stripes.*"*

"Yes," chimed in Private George Fuller, "Show the nice Snapdragon what a real rugged top kick you are."

"There he goes again," said Tech Sergeant Junior Fronk, one of the youngest in the group at 18 years old. "He wants his picture took, the publicity hound." Suddenly Fronk darts out of the column, running abreast of Phil while puffing out his chest. "I eat first sergeants for dinner and I kill lieutenants with my bare hands. I'm Junior Fronk, the hairiest Ranger in the outfit. Take my picture too!" As Torbett shouted for Fronk to get back in the ranks, we doubled over with laughter so that we couldn't run anymore. Fortunately, Captain Roy Murray called "Quick-time!" and the Rangers settled down to easy strides with Phil snapping away like mad and Sergeant Torbett's face redder than hell.

For some reason, possibly because he considered Torbett very photogenic, Stern made Fox Company his adopted outfit. The other companies were a bit peeved because F Company got most of Stern's attention. The men of F Company seemed to feel that it was only logical for Stern to select our men for the most action-packed shots. After all, we were the very best outfit in the battalion. At least that's what we thought. Whenever we got bored with our own tall tales we yanked "Snapdragon" into our tent and challenged him to give out with some colorful stories about Hollywood personalities he had taken pictures of. Stern never let us down. He either was the most sought after photographer in Hollywood or he was the world's best liar.

CHAPTER 3

COLONEL DARBY

Anointed as the father of the modern day Rangers, William Orlando Darby was the first commander to lead the 1st Ranger Battalion during World War II. Darby was revered by his men and respected by his officers and superiors. Described as a born leader, charismatic and confident, he was blessed with movie-star looks and a sleek, strong physique.

At the outbreak of the U.S. entry into the war, Darby was with one of the first troops to deploy to Northern Ireland in January 1942. Promoted to a lieutenant colonel, he worked as an aide to Major General Russell P. Hartle, commander of the 34th Infantry Division.

In the spring of 1942, Brigadier General Lucian Truscott had been tasked with organizing and training the new elite American military unit based on the disciplines of the British Commandos. With a nudge from Hartle, Truscott appointed Major Darby commander of the 1st Ranger Battalion. They would quickly become known as Darby's Rangers. Affectionately nicknamed "Wild Bill" or "El Darbo" by his men, Darby would go on to lead them in campaigns in North Africa, Sicily and Italy.

Phil learned the precise function of the Rangers during his first meeting with the inspirational Colonel Darby. Phil described him as "a strong, handsome guy who is tough as nails and has a great sense of humor."
PHIL STERN

Displaying exceptional leadership and courage, Darby was always conspicuously at the head of his troops, leading the way into battle. He was awarded the Silver Star for his actions in North Africa and twice received the Distinguished Service Cross for his gallantry in the Tunisian Campaign and in Sicily, where Darby repulsed enemy attack, first by destroying an Italian tank using one 37mm anti-tank gun and then by using a heavy machine gun to fight off a counterattack by German tanks. Twice he declined the command of a new infantry combat team in the 45th Division and offer of a full colonelcy from none other than General George Patton. Darby felt he could do more good being with his men. The Rangers believed him to be indestructible, despite his being wounded three times.

In the end, it was a piece of shrapnel from a German 88mm artillery round which pierced his heart and took down the legendary leader. He was just 34 years old when he died, two days shy of the German surrender in Italy. The Rangers' steadfast devotion to their commander continued long after the war ended. Many would visit his family in his home town, sharing stories about Darby and how much they respected him.

The Darby name currently graces Fort Smith, Arkansas, Junior High School where students learn the Ranger Creed, a high school in Cisterna, Italy, U.S. Army installations in Germany and Italy and Camp Darby, near Fort Benning, home to the second part of the Benning Phase of Ranger School. To this day, the high standards, discipline, training and principles set forth 76 years ago continue with each new generation of Army Rangers, keeping the spirit and legacy of Darby alive.

***

SEPTEMBER 26, 1942

My second day at Corker Hill got me a brand new Colt automatic with the pistol belt and 21 rounds of 45 caliber ammunition. I'm proud of my new pistol though I can't even fire the blame thing.

I finally meet Colonel Darby and learn the precise function and meaning of the Ranger organization. It's all quite satisfying and what a thrill to speak with my new "boss." Colonel Darby is a young guy about 31. He'd make any leading man in Hollywood look sick; a strong, handsome guy who is tough as nails and has a great sense of humor. He's from West Point but that's not obvious. You get to respect and like him almost at once. He never

On his second day at Corker Hill Phil proudly handles his brand new Colt Automatic with 21 rounds of 45-caliber ammunition. His new buddies Tony Rada and Denny Bergstrom took turns showing him how to fieldstrip, clean and fire the gun.
PHIL STERN ARCHIVES

beats around the bush and never stops to worry whether his words might hurt anyone's feelings. His job is a grim one and Colonel Darby just isn't going to gum up the works. Gets right to the thick of it.

My meeting with the Colonel is only for a few minutes yet I get all the dope from him as though it were a ten-hour huddle. The First Ranger Battalion was formed with the purpose of being a raiding party - hit and run, spearhead beach landings, harass the enemy and do the rough details which the regular infantry wouldn't have time for. We get lots of rest periods between jobs and always plan and train for new ones. Certainly sounds like the real thing and it's no use kidding anyone. This looks like a game for keeps and I'm beginning to get - not scared but a little worried. Guess there's no use juggling around words. I am a little scared. But I'm going to do my best and besides if anybody gets hit, it won't be me, always the other guy. I'm going to be a walking foxhole or a reasonable facsimile.

   Oh yeah, the old man points out that tomorrow we're starting combat training and there'll be "problems." Also, we're to train with the use of live fire just so that whizzing bullets don't scare us (like hell it don't).

✳✳✳

Private First Class Paul Presley Stroud, Colonel Darby's field clerk, offers a slightly different version of events during Phil's first meeting with Colonel Darby in Altieri's *The Spearheaders.*

Formerly with F Company at Achnacarry, Stroud gave the Rangers the lowdown on Phil Stern, who already was known throughout the battalion by Private George Fuller's choice name, "Snapdragon." Stroud acted out the entire scene for everyone's enjoyment. The lively, peripatetic sergeant, we soon found out, had a most serious mission. Stroud had been in the tent when Stern reported to Darby. He presented his order without very much military courtesy and Darby had curtly straightened him out. Darby then asked Stern why he volunteered for the photographic assignment and what the hell he was going to do with a photographer. Quoting Stern, Stroud recapitulated: "I was in Headquarters in London, living in plush quarters, sitting out the war shooting pictures of generals at social events. It was a good duty but I had a feeling of being nonessential to the war effort. Then I read about volunteers being wanted for the Rangers. Well, sir … I have a belief in our war cause and want to fight it a little more concretely than taking pictures of big shots. Also, I felt that the Rangers would be an outfit whose deeds should be recorded by pictures – a colorful outfit with a colorful commander. And without bragging, it should have its pictures took by the best cameraman in the Army."

"Which, of course, is you," cut in Darby, according to Stroud.

"Yes, sir. I worked for Life *and for some movie mags in Hollywood before the war."*

"That's hardly a recommendation to be a Ranger, Stern. What do you know about soldiering? What do you know about weapons?"

"Frankly, sir, I don't know which end a bullet comes out of a gun, but I can learn."

"You'll also learn how to make a fifteen-mile speed march, how to kill a man with your bare hands. You'll learn how to fieldstrip a rifle blindfolded. We don't want any dead weight around our necks in the outfit."

H.M.S. *Royal Ulsterman*. The Royal Navy transport ships took part in nearly all major Allied amphibious operations of the war in Europe, including Operation *Torch* and the D-Day landings.
© IWM (FL 12259)

"Yes, sir. I'll get the hang of this Ranger stuff, Colonel," Stern bravely ventured.

Whether Stroud had quoted Darby and Stern accurately, we didn't know. Stern, we found later, was a very genial, loquacious fellow.

***

It's hard to believe but in one morning's time I learned how to use the Colt automatic issued to me. Tony Rada and Denny Bergstrom took turns showing me how to field strip the gun and the necessary cleaning measures. Quite fascinating - if only these damn things didn't kill and maim people. But I'm getting off the track. It's

After graduating with honors, the Rangers moved north to Argyll, Scotland, for a month of amphibious training with the Royal Navy. Here they dash across a narrow beach and under barbed wire while running for cover during a landing exercise. Electrically exploded charges helped create a realistic experience.
PHIL STERN

really swell to have pals who will take time out to show a guy these important things and especially when we're just ready to head out for the live fire operations.

We get orders to pack up everything. All personal stuff goes into one barracks bag, properly marked. All battalion equipment gets crated and also marked in heavy paint. Then a file of two and a half ton trucks show up. Orders are hollered out. The whole battalion is to form up, by companies, in front of the vehicles. So all the guys, loaded up with complete shoulder packs, weapon, ammunition and barracks bag, gang around waiting for the next order. Colonel "Wild Bill" Darby comes into the front of all of us. Waves his hand for some quiet. And make no mistake about it, there's not a sound.

"Men," the colonel says, "We're heading for the Glasgow docks where a troop ship is waiting. I want every one calm and no

commotions. Make sure no piece of equipment is left behind. And
don't let your imagination play any tricks. We're going on a
problem. Nothing more." H.M.S. ROYAL ULSTERMAN, that's our ship.
She's a big baby. Not so new but sure is decked out to carry lots
of men and equipment. All the crew and ship complement are
British. We're assigned bunks and mess rooms. Lucky for me to be
a sergeant. All noncoms rate cabins. The other men have to sling
hammocks on the lower decks and call it "home." Later on though,
I discovered that hammocks are lots better than cabin bunks
especially when the ocean isn't too agreeable. So it isn't
always a big bargain to have stripes on your sleeve. For about
four days we just lay in the harbor. All the guys want to get
going. In the meantime we get to pal around with the limey crew.
Get to know the cooks, gunners, landing craft personnel, and the
dozen other specialists for a ship like this. I made friends with
the medical captain of the sick bay. In his cabin was a record
player and his personal collection of Beethoven and Schumann
symphonies. Trouble was that this poor guy was lonely. No one
wanted to listen to Beethoven with all the swing stuff around.
Since I'm sort of ambidextrous and like symphony, the good
doctor gave me a free hand to use his cabin and record collection
any time I please. This certainly helps matters a lot.

One morning we finally we pull out of the harbor. Hardly know
about it because breakfast was being eaten at the time. And what
a breakfast: Fish. The boys call it "one eyes limey fish." Of
course there were really two eyes but since the thing lay on its
side, we could only see one eye. It's pretty tough for Americans
to get accustomed to English food rations and eating customs.
But plenty activity helped offset the thoughts of those meals.
We had calisthenics, weapon cleaning and fire drills. And before
we knew it, our "problem" was on. Our enemy was located on a hill
position. He had big guns covering our beach landing. He had
pillboxes and small gunfire protecting his coastal batteries.
The Rangers objective is to silence those big gun batteries and
shoot up three green flares to indicate that the operation is
successful.

Of course, this is a dry run and we get those flares up into
the sky. Some mistakes were made: faulty communications, a little
confusion on meeting points and some unnecessary noise. Good
lessons are learned. There was a casualty though. Sergeant

A live grenade is tossed dangerously close to a collapsible assault boat as it nears the shore, which
is defended by Commandos. At one juncture, a live grenade was deliberately thrown into a
crammed boat. When it exploded the occupants were already in the water yards away and out of
danger. Split-second thinking was essential.

PHIL STERN

Torbett got a machine gun slug through his right buttock leaving
two holes indicating the bullet's path. From that point on,
Torbett gained overseas fame as being the only sergeant in the
U.S. Army with three assholes.

Our maneuvers continued for several weeks. I learned more and
more about soldiering and weapons. I feel confident and sure of
myself and all my new buddies. I feel that I have a singular and
important job to do in this war. The way Wild Bill puts it he
seems quite flattered that the War Department considers his
battalion important enough to rate a photographer to record the
history of the Rangers. Being a relatively small outfit, I'd
have to pitch it on other details than pure "art." In other

words, some added firepower on my part would help matters. And I am certainly tickled pink to be in a spot like this. Such was my hope from the first day when Uncle Sam got that glint in his eye. And now to make good.

*＊＊

The "problems" Phil refers to was lingo for the unexpected, dangerous obstacles the Rangers would encounter in the pre-invasion assault rehearsal with live ammunition, codenamed "Mosstrooper." On October 13, 1943, the 1st Ranger Battalion boarded a train to Gourock, Scotland. Three former passenger ferries converted into wartime vessels, H.M.S. *Royal Monarch*, H.M.S. *Royal Ulsterman* and H.M.S. *Royal Scotsman* then escorted roughly 500 Rangers per ship ashore via landing craft flotillas for their test. Ranger Jim Altieri described their transport, the *Royal Ulsterman*, as cramped, smelly, dark and uncomfortable, "the flagship of moldy, rust-ridden derelicts in the King's Navy."

Four days of preparations and exercise took place up and down the Firth of Clyde. Safely tucked away from the Atlantic Ocean by the Kintyre peninsula, the Firth of Clyde encloses one of largest and deepest coastal waters in the British Isles.

On October 18 and 19, the final assault exercises began at Loch Linnhe on the west coast of Scotland. Night landings on hostile shores, destroying enemy guns and every type of assault drill imaginable put the Rangers' skills to the test.

The "he" Phil refers to was the pseudo-enemy. The live maneuvers would be a test of what the Rangers would encounter during Operation *Torch*, including rehearsed landings against gun positions and perfecting night-fighting tactics. On October 26 the 1st Ranger Battalion set sail from the River Clyde, accompanied by a convoy of 41 ships.

CHAPTER 4

SHIPPING OUT

OCTOBER 26, 1942. SOMEWHERE IN THE ATLANTIC OCEAN

We had weeks and weeks of intensive training from one island to another in the North Sea. We all got pretty tough and hardened. And we never set foot in Glasgow again. The H.M.S. ROYAL ULSTERMAN slipped back into the Glasgow port, which now is pockmarked with many other ships. Transports — long and skinny ones, short and fat ones, also naval ships, cruisers, battleships and even an aircraft carrier. Smoke was pouring from all the stacks and busy little men could be seen hopping back and forth on all decks. Boy, this is big! Something is cooking, and it sure ain't vegetable soup. It doesn't take long for the news to get around that we are "heading out." Of course, there's no shore leave.

F Company Rangers gather on deck for a group shot as they head to North Africa for their first action of the war. Note the white armbands above the elbow on their left arms, which were used to aid identification at night when the attack began. Officers were to wear them on both arms in order to maintain a level of secrecy during the operation.

PHIL STERN

The next few days are taken up with loading. You'd never think a ship could hold so much stuff. Hundreds and hundreds of crates are hoisted into its holds. These crates are dynamite. They contain ammunitions and high explosives, 30, 40 and 50 caliber shells, 61 millimeter mortar, 80 millimeter, rifle grenades, hand grenades, artillery shells - 75's, 105's and 155's. Then there are mines and Bangalore torpedoes. And to make matters more cheerful, we glance at many tons of various high explosives, such as TNT blocks and firing devices. Of course, ample supplies of chow are piled in too.

At this stage, all parts of the ship are buzzing with whispers. The boys are trying to figure out where we're going. Tony Rada is in the galley with old Sam Oneskunk. They have a map of the world on their knees. Tony says, "I betcha we hit the coast of Norway." Oneskunk grunts. "Or maybe Southern France," says Tony. Oneskunk grunts again. "We might even sock in at the German coast itself," continues Tony. Oneskunk doesn't say a word, but we know damn well he hopes it's South Dakota.

We're five days on the high seas now. It's a big convoy and its direction is quite puzzling because all we do is zigzag. First we head southwest, then southeast and sometimes due north, obviously, to shield our movements from the enemy. Keeps us in the dark too. The men are more than curious; they're hopped up on the matter of destination. Company commanders must constantly inform their men, "We'll let you know soon, boys, take it easy." All our guesses go overboard. All speculations about the French coast, Norway, Germany seem dopey after we learn that our objective is to be the coast of French North Africa. Visions of palms, dates, camels, beautiful Arabian dames fly across my mind. Even lions and tigers and elephants were there. Denny Bergstrom insists I'm all wet. "You'll be lucky to find a jackass much less tigers," he points out.

The next day is set aside by Captain Roy Murray, Commanding Officer of Fox Company, for the enlisted men to get all the dope about our job on the North African shore.

Captain Roy Murray, Jr. and officers of H.M.S. *Royal Ulsterman* give keen study to a detailed model of Port Arzew prior to the North African landings. Use of models, aerial photos and maps ensured that Rangers knew in advance their exact mission and where to expect the most resistance.
PHIL STERN

PREVIOUS PAGES Rangers on board H.M.S *Royal Ulsterman* relaxing after chow time below deck
PHIL STERN

ABOVE On the high seas, en route to North Africa.
PHIL STERN

Meanwhile there isn't too much excitement. A submarine alert is flashed. Nothing happens because one of the Corvettes chases the sub while throwing ash cans (depth charges) all over the place. Our deck gunners don't get the chance of firing. That's how fast it all was. A couple of German planes show up from the west but we're too big a convoy for them to tangle with so they quickly become two even smaller specks in the sky and disappear. All the guys immediately run for the port side railings to watch a school of porpoises ducking in and out of the water while following our ship. Playful little animals I would say.

Four G.I.s show up at the sick bay with scabies. It's not so good getting scabies. Little bugs go on a travel tour all over a guy and make it pretty uncomfortable. What's more it spreads to other men in an awful hurry. The doc, a captain, orders all the men to file past him in single line. These bugs must be stopped and the men with scabies have to be isolated from the rest. It's down on the lower deck and the captain wields one of those G.I. flashlights as he examines this mile long line of naked guys. The doc is a patient worker and doesn't lack a sense of humor. After a few hundred guys get the G.I. flash lamp poked all over them in search of those bugs, the captain suddenly stops, wipes the sweat off his face and to the G.I. next in line he says, "Now isn't this one hell of a way for a guy to make a living?" The G.I. laughs. The whole deck laughs.

In the U.S.A. I often wondered just what soldiers do to kill time on a troop ship. I certainly find out on H.M.S. ROYAL ULSTERMAN. Here's a typical day I spend, and the same goes for most any other guy:

Get woken up by a gong (or the first sergeant when the gong don't work). Have breakfast and immediately run up to the deck to see what kind of day it is and if any land can be sighted. Hang around the rail for a while because the air is fresh and makes you feel good. Then I look around for some close buddies. Bump into Denny Bergstrom and talk about his idea for a new and novel football play. Tony Rada joins in and suggests we swipe some pineapple juice from the galley. By the time the empty Dole can is heaved overboard, we hear the call to deck exercises. For a half hour I bend, jump, sway and limber up. Not bad. Acquire a powerful yen for lunch after which Captain Saam, the demolition man, gives us a "fresher upper" on the proper use of Bangalore torpedoes.

Now it's about time for some stud poker. It's a good game for me. It's a partial release for a lot of nervous energy and gives me a chance to lose some dough I haven't any use for. Also it's a form of social life, which is satisfying. There are groups all around. Some guys are shooting craps. Others go for Blackjack. We don't only gamble. We talk and make cracks about everyone and everything. I drop about sixty bucks by the time evening chow comes up. After chow I try some Blackjack at which I gain pretty near fifty bucks. Gambling gets tiresome and I decide on doing some reading. Aboard this ship it seems that the only books ever published are Ellery Queen mysteries. They're entertaining as well as good time-passers but after reading about ten of them you'll settle for the Rover Boys. The reading problem is solved and I start studying my POCKET GUIDE TO NORTH AFRICA, a pamphlet issued to all the troops a day before. At about 11 p.m. I call it quits and doze off.

That POCKET GUIDE TO NORTH AFRICA is a terrific book. It's got some interesting angles. We all know pretty well about how the Nazis have rolled through one small nation after the other, killing, looting, and generally tearing the town apart in order to terrorize the people into submission. Now get a load of these statements, which are issued officially to American soldiers about to occupy another country. I'm quoting direct from the pamphlets:

When you meet a Moslem he will want to shake hands. Do it gently! Do not pump his hand or squeeze too hard. Many of them, especially the city Moslems, have fine hands which are easily hurt.

A Moslem may even kiss your hand, or raise his fingers to his lips afterward. Do not laugh at him. It is his way of showing politeness.

North Africans, by and large, have an excellent sense of humor. You will not find it difficult to joke with them because they see the humor in situations easily. If they laugh at you, take it; don't get angry. Above all, never strike them.

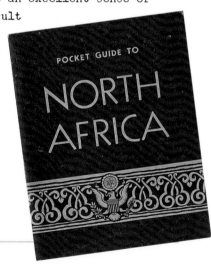

Be kind to beggars. They are mostly honest unfortunates. Give them 25 centimes occasionally if you can spare it.

ABOVE The *Pocket Guide to North Africa* was issued to all Rangers. Appropriate pocket guides would be issued to all American soldiers occupying other countries.
U.S. ARMY

LEFT On the deck of H.M.S. *Royal Ulsterman* Captain Roy Murray, Jr. gathers the Rangers of F Company around him for a briefing. They study the map and go over the fine details of the plan of attack for the impending invasion of North Africa.
PHIL STERN

Be kind and considerate to servants. The Moslems are very democratic.

Avoid any expression of race prejudice. The Moslems draw no color line.

Accept with reserve what local Europeans tell you about North Africans.

Be generous with your cigarettes.

We need the friendship of these people. We need their willing cooperation in maintaining ourselves in their country and we may require their active help in the fight against the common enemy. To be deserving of it, we must treat them with respect and with dignity. Not to do so may make the difference between success and failure in the great undertakings now facing you and fellow Americans.

I never make a lot of noise about patriotism but I feel sort of proud to be in the United States Army.

Two Rangers loaded down and ready for their first major mission: the invasion of North Africa.
PHIL STERN

CHAPTER 5

OPERATION *TORCH*

With the Battle of Stalingrad still raging in the east, the Russians continued to beseech the Allies to open a second front to ease pressure on the Soviet troops from the German forces. While President Roosevelt pressed for a cross-channel invasion of Europe, the British had legitimate concerns regarding the preparedness of American troops to sustain a major invasion.

In a closed-door conference, President Roosevelt, along with Major General George S. Patton, Jr. and Rear Admiral H. Kent Hewitt, decided that an imminent attack on Vichy French-controlled North Africa was the best option. Allied leaders decided on a combined, three-pronged amphibious assault across the North African coast. Beginning on November 8, Major General George S. Patton Jr., with a force sailing from Hampton Roads, Virginia, would hit Casablanca and Morocco; Major General Lloyd Fredendall would lead the center task force at Oran and Arzew; while the British Commandos and U.S. 34th Infantry would land in Algiers to the east.

Rangers weighed down with packs and ammunition, some waiting anxiously, others excited to clash with the enemy on their first big assignment. The main attack at Arzew, North Africa, 1942.

PHIL STERN, SOURCED FROM KEYSTONE-FRANCE/GAMMA-KEYSTONE / GETTY

On October 13, 1942, Operation *Torch* commander General Dwight D. Eisenhower simply explained, "The object of the operations as a whole is to occupy French Morocco and Algeria with a view to the earliest possible subsequent occupation of Tunisia."

Colonel Darby's 1st Ranger Battalion and Major Terry Allen's 1st Infantry Division would come ashore in the critical first wave in a surprise night landing under the cover of darkness in Arzew. Their mission: to seize two coastal batteries defending the entrance of Arzew harbor, a port town near Oran, thus clearing the way for the main landing of the U.S. 1st Infantry Division.

Code-named the "Darby Force," the Rangers would hike up a steep hill, cross a ravine inland and secure the larger gun emplacements at Batterie du Nord overlooking the harbor. The remaining two companies, led by Major Hermann Dammer, would assault three French 75mm gun batteries at Fort de la Pointe.

Naval and air support for the 18,500 ground troops was provided by a British task force of 63 escort vessels: one battleship, three aircraft carriers, three cruisers, 13 destroyers and 43 transports. The main Naval Station at Oran had powerful defenses with 13 coast artillery batteries, 16,700 troops, 100 planes and several destroyers in the harbor.

✳✳✳

NOVEMBER 7-8, 1942, OFF THE COAST OF NORTH AFRICA

It's a beautiful sunny morning on the top deck. The men seem to be in perfect spirits. They're all horsing around while waiting for Captain Roy Murray to show up and give us the skinny about our North African mission. The captain shows up. He's a little guy and not too young but he's wiry and powerful and friendly as they come.

ABOVE LEFT Cruising through rough waters toward the coast of North Africa, Rangers dealt with seasickness by playing poker and practiced calisthenics to release nervous energy on the 13-day journey.
PHIL STERN

LEFT Sailing towards Port Arzew, the 1st Ranger Battalion go over their mission for the invasion of North Africa. United Press correspondent Leo "Bill" Disher, standing in the background, survived 25 wounds from gunshots and shell fragments during Operation *Reservist*, the landing of troops directly into the harbor at Oran in Algeria.
PHIL STERN

With a few hours to go before the mission Father Basil held prayer services on B deck. He heard confessions and gave communion to the Catholics. About a hundred men attend, looking quite solemn.
PHIL STERN

The boys huddle all around him, some sitting right on the deck. Others lean on the rails. A large number just sit around on ammunition boxes. If everyone in on this scene were just three and four feet tall, you would swear it to be in kindergarten with the teacher at the head explaining how to set up blocks. Anyway, Captain Murray gives it to us short and sweet. "We're heading for Port Arzew," he says. This town is in the Oran sector and a large portion of the North African convoy must enter its port. However, there are some powerful coastal gun batteries on the Arzew hills. These guns are four inchers and their muzzles cover the entire town, dock areas, and a few miles of the Arzew waters. Fire from these guns could knock off thousands of men, sink any number of ships and generally hold up our operation.

The guns are supposed to be manned by French naval forces as well as some Foreign Legion units. They may resist strongly. No chances can be taken. The First Ranger Battalion is assigned the task of silencing these gun batteries and capturing its personnel. When that detail is accomplished we're to fire green flares into the sky for the convoy to pour into Arzew harbor. This is a very crucial part of the landing and our battalion is counted on to

clear the path. Captain Murray continued to explain that we will
land at Arzew many hours earlier than any other forces. The
French outnumber us but we will have the advantage because of
the surprise element. Also, we are recently trained and
conditioned whereas the French are garrisoned troops who have
become somewhat lazy from inactivity. This looks like a cinch
and nobody has any kicks coming.

Tonight's the night. We're all like dogs straining at the
leash. There's a nervousness and quiet all over the ship. Most
of the guys are out on the decks going over their maps. Company
commanders drop around and repeat some last-minute instructions.
Each company, each platoon, each squad and each man knows just
what his job is. Here is where some of the finest training will
be tested. This job is all a matter of coordination and cool
thinking. The Port Arzew battle plan amounts to this: A and B
Company will make a direct assault on the docks. Their Higgins
boats have to jump a boom and then head into town via the
extending jetties. This is a rough detail and these two companies
are armed to the teeth: Tommy gunners, B.A.R. men and riflemen.
And they all have plenty of hand grenades. Any mistakes mean the
graveyard for A and B Company. The men of C and D Company will
hit the beach H hour, 1 a.m., November 8, 1942. They must climb
up to the Arzew road running adjacent to the beach. The direction
of the march is east toward the town and docks. C Company will
halt at a point below the French gun batteries and set up their
mortars for actions. D Company must continue on to the town in
order to cover A and B Company who'll no doubt run into trouble.
E and F Company will then jump the boats into the same beach area
as the C and D boys. E and F however don't go to the town. They
will head as close as possible to the gun batteries for the
bayonet attack. Headquarters Company will land with E and F,
coming in with Colonel Darby and his communications men and
runners. I'm to tag along with HQ. We're to set up at a ravine,

---

NEXT PAGES Landing Craft: A morning haze blankets the coast as landing craft carry the 1st
Ranger Battalion eastward to Arzew Bay. Several men were accidently dropped into the sea,
including demolition man Captain Saam, all his explosives, his rifle and a steel contraption for
constricting TNT, called a "beehive." He managed to save his rifle.
PHIL STERN

East of Oran the 1st Ranger Battalion captured a French coastal gun position, along with some 60 prisoners. A soldier in the foreground keeps watch with a machine gun while other soldiers gather in small groups around the gun emplacement. This grainy photo was taken by Phil Stern in the early hours of November 8, 1942.

PHIL STERN

By 4 a.m. the mission to take out the French coastal batteries was successfully executed. Rangers dug in and secured a perimeter of defense around the gun battery, as they stood by for a possible counterattack.

PHIL STERN, SOURCED FROM EVERETT COLLECTION HISTORICAL / ALAMY STOCK PHOTO

With the attack at Fort de la Pointe and Batterie du Nord accomplished, the Navy waited miles offshore for a predesignated signal to offload the 1st Infantry and 1st Armored Division. Because Colonel Darby's white flares had been accidently dumped into the sea, this miscommunication led to a two-hour delay. The 1st Infantry troops finally made their way ashore, missing out on some of the action.
PHIL STERN.

which is at the approaches to the French fort. This ravine is pretty important. From here the whole show will be directed and coordinated. Also the medics are to set up here.

November 7, about 6 p.m.

In a few hours the First Ranger Battalion will be lowered into small landing craft and our mission to Arzew will be on its way. For dinner we have fried chicken with all the extras: potatoes, cranberry sauce and stuff like that. It's a swell meal even if Denny Bergstrom kids us about being fattened up for the kill. I expect to see a lot of nervous guys chewing their fingernails. But it just isn't that way. The boys aren't loud and boisterous as usual. There's a little kidding around a few last minute crap games. The chaplain has a session on B deck. About a hundred guys attend and look quite solemn. I tear ass up to the sick bay. I suddenly discover I have a sore throat and a splitting headache. The doc tells me there's a fever too. And the throat is bogged down with laryngitis. This is a hell of a time to get into such a condition. Doc ties a soft medically treated neckband on me and has me swallow a couple of pills. Then he says try not to get wet. Isn't that a smart crack for the books? How's a guy going to keep dry on a beach landing? The medic smiles a little but I guess I feel too lousy to appreciate his humor. Everything's working like a charm. It's pretty near 12 a.m. now. Men are quietly shuffling around the decks. All companies are assembling at their boat stations. Sergeants are making sure none of their men are missing. Verbal orders can be heard well even though no one is yelling. The British crewmen are quietly tending their posts awaiting orders to lower the landing craft. Wish we'd start moving.

It's our turn now. Over the rail and into the suspended boats. We're all in except for Captain Saam. Now he makes it and decides to lie on the craft's edge instead of hopping inside. Pulleys lower away. About 15 feet from the water something snaps. There's a big splash and we're bounced around. The guys' helmets and guns clattering against each other but what a break. The flat bottom keeps us in the water. It's a close one, but where in hell is Captain Saam? We're looking out into the black water and sure enough there's Saam bobbing up and down. He loosened his pack and rifle and sent them to Davey Jones. Lucky for him that he didn't fall between our craft and the ship or he'd certainly end up a hamburger. We pull out our wet captain. The delay only amounts to about five minutes. The motors churn and now we head for shore.

It's a calm Mediterranean. Smooth, black sky, cloudless and plenty of stars, which are our only light because it's about a 1/20th moon, the size of a Schrafft's* slice of apple pie, and doesn't throw off enough light to write home about. It's a low huddle for all of us. There's no use describing my thoughts during this little cruise. I relived my lifetime in that little craft and it would take a dozen books to tell about it.

---

*   Schrafft's was a chain of high-volume moderately priced New York restaurants known for their desserts, candy and apple pie.

12:45 a.m.

Right on the nose! We sight the black outline of the North African coast. Hard to believe but it's there. Boy it's going to be a luxury to put our feet on land again. Captain Saam is shivering a bit and don't get me wrong, it's not from fright. He isn't dry yet. We can practically reach out and touch Africa now. One of the boats bangs into a rock near the beach. The men are up to their shoulders in water. Some are swimming but they make it for the sand. The lead boat flashes us the signal not to hit the beach until a clear area is located. Doesn't take long for the all-clear flash. There's a dull crash, the craft's mouth opens and it looks just as though men and guns are just spat out on to the beach. We're lucky. Just up to the waist in water. The water is refreshing and comfortably warm. No shore fire. Jesus, those guys must be asleep. Or maybe they're waiting till we get further up the beach.

None of us intends to dilly dally on the beach so we scramble inland. Doesn't take long for the soft sand to disappear and we hit hard, rocky ground going uphill. We're a hundred yards inland now and still no fire. Our rubber-soled shoes against the rocks make quite a racket or perhaps it's so quiet that sound waves are confusing. An officer up front orders a halt. The word passes down quietly to all of us. I hit the ground and wait. My 45 is loaded and on half cock. It's so dark I can't figure out who the guys beside me are. And there's no time for light conversation. We hop to our feet again and this time there's a

---

ABOVE LEFT Vichy troops surrender. Taken by surprise, the battery commander officer had barely enough time to grab his coat and cap. A comedy of errors ensued when Darby allowed the officer to meet him at dawn to formally surrender. Instead, a burst of enemy machine gun fire rained in on the Rangers' positions. Darby was as mad as hell. Via radio he relayed a threat of mortar and Navy gunfire. The French commander quickly acceded.
PHIL STERN

LEFT According to Phil, the Vichy commandant was a burly French naval officer who looked and acted like the Austrian actor Eric von Stroheim – well-known for playing sneering villains with a comical Prussian dialect and eccentric mannerisms. To the Rangers the commandant was "sourpussed and sullen;" his honor had clearly been smitten.
PHIL STERN

TOP "Commandant" Phil. With his camera pack, notepad and gun at the ready, Phil takes a short break on the French outpost at the entrance to the French commandant's lair in Arzew on the first day of the invasion.

PHIL STERN ARCHIVES

ABOVE Phil, a couple of Rangers, a French officer and Royal Navy sailors pose in front of the "Artillerie de Cote," the entrance to the heavy coastal artillery, defensive guns and antiaircraft weapons at Batterie du Nord.

PHIL STERN

LEFT Fort du Nord. The mission was to attack two separate coastal batteries at Arzew. Fort de la Pointe was located on the harbor's edge, on a hill overlooking the harbor. Batterie du Nord was a four-gun battery equipped with long-range rifles. Darby's decision to split the 1st Ranger Battalion with Major Dammer resulted in a one–two punch.

PHIL STERN

steep rocky hill to climb. B.A.R. gunners are already at the hilltop covering our movement. In a few minutes we hit upon a beautiful paved road. Colonel Darby is here. He's asking questions and giving orders over the walkie-talkie. Firm but quietly the Colonel finishes and we march single file, one file each side of the road, toward Arzew and the ravine. The men are twenty feet apart and ready for anything. Two mutts start barking, high shrill woofs. Must be French poodles. It's distracting as hell. I'd like to strangle them. We're high on the road now. There's houses outlined against the ocean. I wonder if any people are home. Damn those mutts. Shots ring out from the dock area. A and B must be getting it in Dutch. Seems like a lot of guys are overlapping other guys. I get quite confused. There's a short break. I hop into a gully alongside the road. There's a guy next to me and I ask him if I'm still with Headquarters. "Hell no," he says. Turns out I'm with C Company and this guy says stick around and watch some fancy mortar firing. Having no other social engagements I hang around. Firing continues from the town and docks. I can hear Tommy guns, rifle fire and some distant machine gun sputtering. My pal wasn't kidding about the mortars. My eyes are now better accustomed to the dark and I find myself on the side of the road with a mortar crew. There's about a half dozen riflemen down the road to take care of disturbers. It'd be corny to say that mortar fire sounds like whoosh, whoosh. But that's what it's like. Our mortars are shot up into the gun batteries. There's a flash and you hear the concussion. I feel sorry for anybody within thirty yards of where these babies land. We keep throwing them, directed by Colonel Darby from his walkie-talkie of course. There's plenty of flashes and crashes interspersed with small arms fire from the town. Mortars quit. Must be waiting for the bayonet assault on the gun batteries. Yep. With howls and screams and a terrific racket, the assault group makes for the gun positions. Sounds like a scene from a cowboy and Indian movie. What teamwork! In practically no time at all we can see the green flares shoot up into the sky. That means the ships can move in closer to shore without fear of fire. My watch says 4:30 a.m. Time sure is running a hundred yard dash. Soon it starts getting light and I'm on my way up the hill to the French fort. The tough climbing should be quite a sight.

Those big guns are four inchers, German made and are painted

in orange and black camouflage. They've been dug in solidly in
concrete pits. The boys are all over the guns and it's like old
home week. Everybody's meeting their pals. No one's knocked off
yet. A few guys are laid up with bullet wounds. Part of A and B

ABOVE When the enemy barricaded themselves into an underground powder magazine, a large
party of Rangers rammed through the entrance of Batterie du Nord. Grenades and a Bangalore
torpedo were pushed down the ventilators, following which 60 prisoners came out with their
hands in the air. The eclectic group consisted of French Legionnaires, Germans, Moroccans and a
Jewish man with an uncle in Brooklyn.
PHIL STERN

NEXT PAGES After close combat during the early morning hours, the Rangers secured Fort du
Nord, which they learned was also used as a convalescent home for the French Foreign Legion.
A lone Ranger stands guard above the entrance, built into the mountain. With the coast cleared, a
truck leaves through the entrance.
PHIL STERN

PREVIOUS PAGES Having taken over respective gun positions without incident, Rangers Lodge and Altieri checked out a dozen dugouts near captured gun positions. In total they apprehended 70 French soldiers, some half-dressed, shocked and anxious to surrender, while others were reportedly indignant when caught with a prostitute.
PHIL STERN

ABOVE By the end of the day, approximately 300 prisoners had been captured. This included North African and Senegalese *tirailleur* regiments of the French Army of Africa.
PHIL STERN

Company reached the gun positions and boy! Were they woozy. My pal Murray from B Company says the docks were loaded with hundreds of jumbo sized French wine barrels and they weren't filled with banana oil. An advance group shot into town and the other guys fired their automatics into the lower regions of the wine barrels. The red stuff poured out. And like good Rangers our boys imbibed. They loaded their canteens with the same fluid and specially appointed runners saw that the advance squads were properly taken care of. No one can really call this looting because the wine was scheduled for shipment to Germany. The big payoff is that about two dozen Rangers, saturated with vin rouge, climbed the hill to the big gun emplacements and made the frontal assault without loss to a single man.

***

After climbing over a seawall and cutting through barbed wire, two groups of Rangers under Major Dammer assaulted Fort de la Pointe from opposite directions. Within 15 minutes, they had the fort and 60 startled French prisoners. Meanwhile, Darby and the remaining four companies successfully reached Batterie du Nord and with the support of Company D's four 81mm mortars the force assaulted the position, capturing the battery and 60 more prisoners. The operation was going exactly according to plan.

***

What a bunch of characters I get tied up with. We're examining the French gun pits and admiring the beautiful mortar work, which hit within five and ten yards of the actual guns. That's good shooting. The prisoners are all lined up by now and Captain Martin is directing the tagging of our prisoners and they are a jumbled assortment of people: lots of French Legionnaires, a couple of Germans, some Moroccans, a Dutchman, a Frenchman and a Jew who has an uncle in Ocean Park in Brooklyn. The Commandant is a burly Frenchman who looks and acts like the Austrian actor Eric Von Stroheim. His chest fully inflated, this particular French officer is sourpussed and sullen. His honor has been smitten. He claims that if he didn't have such a lazy, fat bunch of oafs under his command he could've put up resistance of a more effective nature. Colonel Darby feels for him and in so many words offers him a TS (tough shit) card to be punched by the chaplain.

The 18th Infantry is now moving in from the eastern outskirts of Arzew. Some snipers and machine gun nests are slowing the move up. Colonel Darby sends C Company down into town to draw some of the fire. I tag along with C. We let loose with rifle fire. Some snipers return fire. The resistance is terribly disorganized – it only takes a few hours to clean up.

The French garrison paid lots of attention to their eating and conveniently maintained an elaborate network of chicken coops. It didn't take long for our hillbilly cook, Jim Teague, to bayonet a few birds and set them up on the fire. What a contrast

ABOVE From a strategic vantage point above the port town of Arzew, Ranger Corporals Robert Bevan and Earl Drost engaged snipers barricaded in warehouses along the waterfront. The attack was so swift that by dawn all the terrain was occupied before the French realized what had happened. Shortly after this picture was taken, the town capitulated.

PHIL STERN

LEFT Corporal Robert Bevan, E Company, on the left with the M1903 Springfield, had to have good eyes and a steady hand to be a sniper using open sights. Corporal Earl Drost came from the original A Company crew of the 168th Regiment of Iowa. They were all farmers who had no idea their service would become so significant.

PHIL STERN

ABOVE LEFT Basking in the thrill of victory during their first night raid, several Rangers look over Arzew and the Mediterranean Sea while posing for an action shot with a captured French gun.
PHIL STERN

LEFT Examining a French gun pit, Phil and fellow Rangers pose with Schnopsie, one of the stray dogs roaming around Arzew. Ranger Ben Temkin noted the dog could hear an air raid coming well before anyone else had any warning and would dive under a vehicle. Rangers learned to follow his lead.
PHIL STERN

TOP Phil and fellow Rangers pose atop a French armored car in Arzew. Taken by surprise and lacking organization, the majority of French batteries were out of action by daylight.
PHIL STERN

TOP Ranger mortars. A well-planned and well-aimed mortar barrage led by D Company was key to capturing the French guns with few casualties.
PHIL STERN

ABOVE Basking in the successful capture of Batterie du Nord, Phil wasn't satisfied until he had his favorite model, First Sergeant "Butt" Torbett, pose with his arms around a four-inch gun as though the sergeant himself had captured the battery unaided.
PHIL STERN

to the field rations we carried, which consisted of meat and beans, hard tack, G.I. coffee and the D-ration chocolate bars. Now for some chow so we head back to the fort where, believe it or not, there's fried chicken and red wine.

***

AFTER ACTION REPORT

Operation *Torch* marked the largest amphibious operation attempted in the history of modern warfare to date. The Rangers were America's first foot soldiers to fight in North Africa and later Europe. Considered the first major land victory of the Allied powers, the operation boosted troops' morale and began turning the tide of the war in the Allies' favor. Newly opened ports allowed ships and equipment to move more easily for future campaigns and raids along the coast of Africa, into Sicily and eventually to mainland Italy and Europe.

Two ill-conceived late additions in the planning phase, codenamed Operation *Reservist* and Operation *Terminal*, were deemed failures. Both involved the direct landing of infantry into Vichy French ports before they could be destroyed. The *Reservist* force assaulted Oran harbor and the British-led *Terminal* was to enter Algiers harbor on two Royal Navy destroyers, debark and secure port facilities. Expecting a surprise landing, Allied ships instead came in under sustained fire from 31 French ships. 189 out of 393 American infantrymen were killed in the *Reservist* action, along with 113 British dead and 86 wounded. *Terminal* casualties numbered 22 killed and 55 wounded, and all landed infantry were captured.

For the Rangers, their first operation as an independent unit was successfully executed with few casualties. The 1st Ranger Battalion had established itself as a formidable American fighting force and duly celebrated with captured barrels of French wine.

NEXT PAGES Rangers at the ready in dugouts in Arzew during Operation *Torch*.
PHIL STERN

CHAPTER 6

OCCUPATION ARZEW

NOVEMBER 9, 1942, ARZEW AND ORAN

Fort du Nord turns out to be a comfortable home for us even though we have to pull out to other quarters in a couple of days. The country out here is plenty picturesque. Rolling hills, which are green and rocky. Art Spack of C Company comes from Butte, Montana, and says North Africa is a lot like his home state in terrain and coloring. To me it's like Arizona and Southern California. The little houses are very light colored and definitely constructed along different architectural lines than American homes. These places are mostly villa-like and have courtyards with chickens and pigs bivouacked on the grounds and even inside the rooms. C Company seems to be given the rough end of most details. The whole company, commanded by Lieutenant

Breaking bread with locals. "Arabs are some of my favorite people,"
said Phil of his newfound friends. According to Phil's wartime memoir, they learn fast and
are alert to any funny situation or a gag.
U.S. ARMY

ABOVE AND LEFT Colonel Darby made good use of his Harley-Davidson WLA Liberator motorcycle speeding from one end of Arzew to the other, directing the entire operation, the aftermath and days following. Phil apparently saw "El Darbo" give hell to a full colonel for not moving his men across the beach fast enough.

PHIL STERN

Kleftman, was ordered to defend the First Division command post in the village of Tourville, then knock out French 75s at St. Cloud. These guns were holding up the American advance into Oran, twenty miles away. Our boys did their job well but Lieutenant Kleftman and three of his men were killed by direct shellfire. Father Basil led the services for them at a make-shift cemetery at Les Andalouses, near Algiers atop Arzew harbor. The white crosses overlook the very waters these men plied across just less than two days ago. It's a sad occasion but we move on.

***

In the aftermath of the successful invasion at Oran a group of Rangers were sitting a half mile above the harbor watching the operations unfolding at the port. Jim Altieri writes in *The Spearheaders* what happened next.

Phil Stern bounded up the hill. Grinning, he carried the booty of war in the form of a German Leica camera dangling from a neck strap and a bulky canvas bag crammed with rolls of captured film slung over a shoulder. Having shot several rolls of Rangers in action, from their landings to the seizure of their objectives, he demanded his favorite subject, Butt Torbett, pose hugging the barrel of one of the four-inch guns "Listen, fellows" he said dramatically, "These pictures will soon be seen by millions of people back home. These pictures will tell the story of what we Rangers accomplished in opening the gates for the attack on Oran."

During a meeting of F Company and "El Darbo" at the Former Foreign Legion Convalescence facility, Altieri recalled Phil barging in waving copies of the Army newspaper *Stars and Stripes* and a three-week-old *New York Times*. "The whole country knows about Arzew. Look! My pictures!" exclaimed a very excited Stern. The headline from *Stars and Stripes* read:

DARING RANGERS SILENCE COASTAL GUNS
CRACK NIGHT FIGHTERS TAKE ARZEW ON D-DAY
THEN SMASH WAY TO ORAN

"Stern's pictures," wrote former Altieri in *The Spearheaders,* "had not only made the public aware of the Rangers but they had given us a new surge of pride and spirit at a crucial time when many were beginning to doubt the wisdom of joining the Rangers and felt disappointment that they were not being used for Commando raids as they had envisioned."

ABOVE RIGHT Ranger gunners in a foxhole man antiaircraft ack-ack guns while scanning the skies for enemy planes after the landings in North Africa, November 1942.
PHIL STERN

RIGHT Rangers take a well-deserved rest along the jetties in the harbor. Despite losing a radio to the Mediterranean at the outset, the attacks on the Arzew batteries were carried out exactly as planned. Casualties were fairly light: the Rangers suffered four killed and 11 wounded. Colonel Darby would preside as the town mayor of Arzew.
PHIL STERN

NEXT PAGES Rangers perform a cleanup on the beach after the fight for the port of Arzew a day after the attack on November 11, 1942. The invasion was the first time the original battalion was in combat as a unit. Training would resume promptly a day later.
PHIL STERN

Appointed as the new military mayor of Arzew, Colonel Darby dealt with non-battle issues such as providing water and electricity to the town, whether to open the local bordello, and where to bury the dead. Here, he briefs senior staff outside the city hall on upcoming Tunisian operations.
PHIL STERN

***

The new headquarters of the First Ranger Battalion is the Arzew City Hall, located in the center of town. We share the place with the local French authorities. These people have plenty of headaches. They must regulate the food ration system. They work on passports for people who may want to visit a town just twenty miles away. And of course they have no easy time with the Gendarmes who must watch the black market, take care of drunks and constantly bawl out the bad girls who insist on being overly affectionate to Americans in payment with chocolate bars.

We set up our own Military Police to take care of traffic and of occasional G.I.s who absorb a little too much vin rouge. The key to our relation with the French turns out to be Private Roy Anctil, a New York man who ran an ambulance service on the West Side. Roy spent many years in Southern France and rattled off the lingo just as good as the Mayor of Arzew. Anctil was a bit stumped when it came to gabbing with the Arabs but he managed with a few French words and some well put gestures with the arms. Poor Roy never got any sleep. Many times he had to iron out little rough

ABOVE Hoping to get some good action shots, Phil tagged along with an assault section assigned to clean out snipers on the outskirts of town near Oran. Moving up the street, slugs tear into a nearby wall just over Phil's head. U.S. Rangers rake all the windows along the street with Tommy-gun and rifle fire, then kick down the door of a questionable building.
PHIL STERN, SOURCED FROM INTERFOTO / ALAMY STOCK PHOTO

NEXT PAGES Mortar men get their weapons ready for battle in the rugged Tunisia Mountains following the successful *Torch* landings.
PHIL STERN

ABOVE LEFT Private First Class Charles Diehl of E Company, 1st Battalion, barters with a local for an orange. Bartering with the Arabs was a popular pastime in North Africa. Not all Rangers were as successful as Diehl. He was later wounded during the Sened Station Raid in Tunisia.
PHIL STERN

ABOVE RIGHT Chaplain Albert E. Basil, on loan from the British Commandos, leads a group prayer for the fallen U.S. soldiers in Arzew. Four C Company Rangers were the first to be killed in action, with eight wounded, when they came under intense fire from a French strongpoint at La Macta during a night march near St. Cloud. They were buried in a temporary cemetery at Les Andalouses, near Algiers.
PHIL STERN

spots like where some French gal would insist that a certain G.I. promised to marry her and is now welching. Arzew is a close knit little town with no more than three thousand people, mostly Arabs and French. I'm sure that brother Roy Anctil knows them all personally. And as a compensating factor, there are a number of pretty French gals in town and only Roy can talk to them. All the G.I.s were on his tail for introductions. Me too.

The Arabs are my favorite people. They learn things fast and are very alert to a funny situation or a gag. I suppose that's from years of living by their wits. I can't forget the ugly, rainy day I picked to visit my Signal officer in Oran. Cold, rainy and I'm in an ugly mood. The trip to Oran in a jeep is a bouncing affair. The roads aren't too level and I have to pass through St. Cloud and see all the bullet-spattered buildings where C Company caught hell. There's one traffic jam after another in the center of Oran. I almost skid into about five or six Arab goat carts which somehow are always swerving on to the wrong side of the street. I finally make Signal headquarters. Still raining hard (did I say this country is like California?) so I remained in my seat to rest and wait for a dry spell. I can hear an Arab to the rear of me urging his donkey onwards. He makes some funny noises which are the equivalent of our "Giddyap!" I mimicked the Arab by repeating his sounds. When the cart rolled some thirty feet away the Arab turned his head back toward me and bellowed out, "Blow it out your ass, Joe!"

You see these Arabs are really on the ball. We've only been in Africa about five days and he picked just the right kind of English to take care of a guy who makes fun of him. I get a big laugh out of this incident and develop a much brighter outlook toward my Signal Corps chore and the lousy day I pick to do the job.

On the way back to Port Arzew I discover a very interesting social phenomena. On the outskirts of Oran there's a red light district, which is run strictly G.I.* The women are French and Arabs and are carefully inspected by our medical officers. This whorehouse area occupies a street about four New York City blocks long. At each end of this avenue M.P.s are on guard. Naturally there are a lot of G.I.s who merely wish to walk through this street and observe the houses, the lines of guys, and perhaps catch a quick look at the females so they might tell of their colorful experience when they get back home. Now the M.P.s have orders to send all soldiers to the prophylaxis station for treatment even if the poor guy was just on a sight-see. So the G.I. tourist gets caught on his way out and must take a "pro" treatment. Some of them sullenly walk off to the "pro" station while some others run back to the whorehouses for a fast visit. I believe the Army is very intelligent being so scientific about the existence of whorehouses. In any case, the venereal disease rate is cut down a big chunk.

Back at Arzew I learn of new orders for the battalion to move. No action. We've got an extensive training program ahead. Our new

---

*   The expression "strictly G.I." means that the brothel was run only for U.S. soldiers.

ABOVE Their first combat mission deemed a success, the Rangers now considered themselves experienced soldiers and deserving of some rest and relaxation. Darby made sure his men did not rest on their laurels. Wasting little time, he immediately began training his men harder than before with speed marches on rugged terrain and climbing steep cliffs. The main focus was on amphibious landings under every conceivable condition, and small unit tactics.
PHIL STERN

bivouac area is right on the beach about two miles out of Arzew. It's really a super duper arrangement, quite unusual for the Army. We don't live in tents at all because this beach happens to be a resort area visited by the middle class French during the summer months. Of course it's wintertime now and the war has stranded the occupants all over cosmopolitan France and the French colonial cities in North Africa. But there's still just about enough villas to absorb our battalion. I suppose it's natural for people to

ABOVE LEFT A welcome rest period allows Darby to do some personal grooming and cleaning up on the beach in Arzew. Not only was he a strong leader, he was also known to be a superb dancer with a good singing voice.
PHIL STERN

ABOVE RIGHT On the morning of the third day, the French capitulated to the Allies. Assuming they were heading out on yet another speed march, First Sergeant Torbett instead led F Company to Beach Red in Arzew. Here the sweaty, naked and cursing Rangers jump in the cool Mediterranean Sea, washing off the grime and stink of three days. Two locals strolling along the beach don't seem to mind.
PHIL STERN

desire a pleasant place to return to after a hard day's work. That goes for soldiers too. Our weeks of training at Arzew are strenuous and nerve wracking but at least we come home to a cheerful little house on the Mediterranean. There's often time for an afternoon swim. That guy wasn't kidding when he said, "The Blue Mediterranean." This ocean is blue, warm and clean. I'm five foot eleven and I can see my toes while treading water.

Colonel Darby encouraged the idea of bathing at the beach because the men would horse around, getting plenty of exercise

Colonel Darby lights a cigarette for Major General Terry de la Mesa Allen. The colorful commander of the 1st U.S. Infantry Division was born on an Army post into a family with strong military traditions. A World War I vet, Allen served on the Western Front at St. Mihiel and Aincreville. In October 1944 he took command of the crack 104th Infantry Division "Timberwolves," the first unit to reach the Elbe River and link up with the Soviet Red Army.
PHIL STERN

and get a cleaning at the same time. The Colonel himself made a habit of going for a dip every morning before chow. He is the only man to do it because it's quite cold in the mornings and the water isn't any too welcome. But that didn't bother Wild Bill. He and his blue Jantzen trunks made a beeline for the water in spite of the elements. He'd come out shivering which would give everybody a laugh. We don't laugh too loud.

Mess out on the beach is okay until there's a sand storm at which time every dish is served à la sand. It's remarkable how our food habits change with new conditions of living. We eat mutton with sand and don't mind at all. We smoke cigarettes, drop ashes in our coffee, drink the coffee. Our boys are really hardened by now.

Our training consists of speed march after speed march across sand dunes, over hills and mountains. We also go on "problems." Street fighting, storming gun batteries, amphibious landings and other such items. We get a few new weapons and there's plenty practices and training with them. The high command must certainly have some special plans for the Rangers. Anyway this constant training puts us all in fine physical condition. The boys are tough physically and practically never catch colds or other ailments you get when you're a fat lush.

My job with the Rangers is essentially a photographic one. Up to this point I've already taken hundreds of photos of all our activities. I don't mention much about my photography. Maybe it's because it is my trade and I'm reluctant to talk shop. On many occasions it's a definite advantage to be a photographer. Particularly when Garnett gets an amphibious jeep from the motor pool and convinces Colonel Darby of the necessity for testing the vehicle for its strategic possibilities. Of course, I insist on the importance of recording this testing by means of pictures. So "Blackie," (that's the nickname the guys gave him due to his hair color) loads on some small boxes, strategic gear I guess, and we take off. This gadget is really something, definitely a motorboat on wheels. "Blackie" drives. We put about three miles off where we're in such a spot that the guys on shore can just barely see us. This boy "Blackie" is a genius. He opens the boxes and the contents are quite non-strategic. It's a fishing tackle, spam sandwiches and French wine. There's no fish to catch but it's a lot of fun trying. And the picnic lunch makes the occasion a still happier one.

In fairness to "Blackie" it should be said that he is more than a mere promoter. He is considered the battalion Romeo. A pretty French girl visits our orderly room almost every day to demand that "Blackie" be forced to make good his promise of marrying her. Many times this gal even brings along her whole family. "Blackie's" problem is to duck her when these visits take place. That's where being transportation sergeant helps.

A very definite contribution to the Allied war effort is a little Arabian boy called Achmed. He's a spry and alert kid who is madly in love with our G.I. "chawcalott" rations. Sourball candy is okay too but secondary. Achmed's good fortune is that his folks live in a hut along our usual line of speed marches.

It's a break for us too because Achmed trails along on our hikes and when one of our guys reaches the breaking point, our little Arabian pal takes over the G.I.'s gear and lugs it for a reasonable period of time and in return gets a bar of "chawcalott." Achmed is shrewd enough to pick a proper place for his operations. That part of the column farthest away from the company commander. His business flourished to the point where he hired some pals and paid them on a commission basis. It's never a surprise for us to see some half pint Arab kid marching in cadence with a Browning Automatic Rifle across his back and a G.I. in front of him with a silly grin on his puss.

I must tell about one of our humanitarian company commanders. He's a first class infantry officer and full of surprises. While finishing one of our more strenuous hikes and passing through Arzew he suddenly changes his character and says, "Okay men. We're going to continue in real Fort Dix style. Strictly G.I. and in drill formation." Naturally we're all surprised at this and make no secret of our displeasure. So we do it according to book. That is, until we reach Arzew's leading Brasserie, or beer joint. The captain hollers, "Company Halt!" right alongside of the joint, then says, "Company dismissed and don't drink too much of that beer!"

One warm night while sitting around a bonfire on the Arzew beach, Captain Bill Martin comes over to us and gives us the low down on his recent trip to Casablanca and Spanish Morocco. It was a secret mission and I never found out the purpose for the intelligence Captain's trek to Morocco. In any case I wanted to

ABOVE LEFT Workers at the port of Oran fleeing during the German bombing of Algiers harbor following the successful Allied occupation.
PHIL STERN

LEFT Dressed in fatigues and loaded down with full battle equipment, F Company Rangers packed into assault boats, ferrying them to shore for a mock beach landing. Their temperamental craft, manned by an ill-prepared coxswain from the 36th Engineer Amphibious Brigade, spun around and headed towards the beach ass-backwards, ramming into a sand bar 40 yards from shore. As ramps opened men were dumped into the water up to their armpits, forced to carry their rifles overhead. Junior Fronck went under and had to be piggybacked on to the beach. Darby stated this was the most fouled up landing he'd ever seen and sent them back to start all over again.
PHIL STERN

know what's cooking in Casablanca. Martin lets us know by getting right to the point. "The boys in Casa," says the Captain, "are sitting on their cans waiting for shipment east. To pass the time away they have put together a song which they sing all the time. It's called 'Stella from Fedala'." I'd like to repeat the complete lyrics but believe me, it's a highly censorable ditty which even this book would blush at were it in print. Anyway it starts like this:

Now every young Yank who was in Casablanca
Knows Stella, the belle of Fedala.
A can of C-rations will whip up a passion
In this little gal of Fedala

This epic is sung to the tune of "Abdallah Bulbul Ameer." You'll have to figure this out for yourself.

Meat and Beans à la Francais

It's quite a feat to get a decent meal in the town of Arzew. These people have been milked dry by the Germans. Seems as though the Arzew folks thrive on fish, rationed dark bread and red wine. My solution to this problem is really a very simple one. On a trip to town I bring along a can of G.I. meat and beans. I sit at the table and when the waitress comes over she gets the can. And back in the kitchen the chef goes to work. The result is a warm, delicious dish of meat and beans prepared à la Francais with all the proper seasoning. Some red wine added to this makes a very tasty meal. These French are an ingenious people when it comes to food. All they have to have is the ingredients.

ABOVE RIGHT Rangers sightseeing from the top of a mini pyramid in Arzew.
PHIL STERN

RIGHT Phil chowing down on a hearty meal. "Mess out on the beach is okay until there's a sand storm at which time every dish is served à la sand," he commented in his memoir. His recipe for a decent meal: mixing a can of G.I. ration meat and beans then sending it to the chef, who adds seasoning and red wine, and *voilà!* Meat and Beans à la Francais.
U.S. ARMY

In late November, the 1st Ranger Battalion was stationed near the 48th Surgical Nurses' barracks. Appointed to escort the nurses between their quarters and the hospital, the Rangers guarded all gates, prohibiting other men from visiting. "We were dating all the Rangers and they were just great!" later recalled Lieutenant Helen Moloney.

PHIL STERN

Rangers hoped to convert the French military to the Allied cause by introducing them to the favorite American pastime of baseball. They showed them how to hold and swing a bat like Joe DiMaggio.

PHIL STERN

Major William Darby dining with the some of his men during chow time in Tunisia in February 1943. The Brown Derby sign was T-5 James Smiley's idea. He hailed from West Virginia and was also his outfit's cook. He had fond memories of the Brown Derby restaurant just around the corner back home.
PHIL STERN

I believe that one of the greatest crimes the Germans have perpetuated on the French was to abort their food supply. Anyway, my conscience is clear. By supplying my own meat and beans I don't deplete the already meager French supply of chow.

A guy certainly acquires an education by getting overseas. In the States I couldn't understand a word of French. I now have a fluent knowledge of about six French phrases. I can ask a French man very glibly, "How are you? Care for a cigarette? How much?" For more romantic purposes I can say, "You are very pretty. How about strolling through the park?" French is a pretty language. Wish I could get time off to really study it. The latest phrase I picked up is, "Where is the men's room, please?" This one comes in awful handy.

An interesting institution in Oran is one of the public bathhouses. After a while it becomes a necessity to visit one of these joints. My favorite is the "Baines Cavaiguac." Firstly, I always meet a lot of old friends here who also need a rinsing. Secondly, the rates are quite low. "Simple Bain" - 9 francs. "Le Bain Turc" - 10 francs, "Douche" - 8 francs. The "Douche" is okay for me, just a plain shower. I don't even know what the others mean. The operation involved has only two drawbacks for the beginner. The plumbing is marked "chaud" and "froid." You can freeze or get burnt by turning the wrong knob. And the water is loaded with African minerals and you must suffer to get any lather from your bar of Lifebuoy.

The Headquarters Bulletin Board always has news of great import to the First Ranger Battalion. Mostly of a military nature. Training schedules, new G.I. directives, promotions, changes in company command, etc. Sometimes we'll find another type of notice where a guy announces that he lost his wallet and that the finder may keep all the dough just so long as he returns the snapshot of the wife and baby. For a gag, Denny Bergstrom once tagged the following notice on to the Bulletin Board: "Lost. My 3-A draft card. Please return. Liberal reward."

An example of Colonel Darby's sense of humor is shown by a letter he personally put on the bulletin board. The President of the Boy Rangers of America sent Colonel Darby the following v-letter:

I am very anxious to make the acquaintance of our Big Brother Rangers overseas. Upon receipt of this letter please write and tell us your experiences in Africa and we will assign one of your little Ranger brothers to tell you of our doings.

Yours for Victory,
Trusty Tommy

This Junior Ranger business has its value too. On occasions where a Ranger would botch his detail or fail to follow out an important order, his commanding officer would lose no time at all in threatening a transfer to the Boy Rangers of America. Don't think that this doesn't have an immediate positive effect.

"REAL AFRICAN SAND HONEST!"

FRENCH NORTH AFRICA
JAN 15, 1943

DEAR HARRIET,
YOUR V LETTER JUST BLEW IN ON A GUST OF AFRICAN WIND. THANX A LOT. A GUY ALWAYS LIKES TO HEAR FROM THE PEOPLE HE LIKES. I'M STILL IN NORTH AFRICA AND ITS VERY EXCITING TOO. I MEET A LOT OF ARAB AND FRENCH PEOPLE. TOO BAD I CANT SPEAK FRENCH.

HERE ARE SOME INSIGNIAS. REPRESENTS A COUPLE OF CITIES IN FRANCE. HOPE YOU LIKE 'EM

COQ DE FRANCE

MOM AND VICK ARE IN LOS ANGELES AND VICK IS ACTUALLY IN THE "PITCHERS"! I'LL BET YOU'RE PRETTY PROUD OF YOUR COUSIN.

I HOPE YOU DONT MIND ME PUTTING THOSE INSIGNIAS AND SILLY DRAWING ON THE LETTER.

BEST WISHES TO MOM, POP, ~~LEE~~, LOU, AND JOJO,

Phil

P.S. TELL MOM I JUST GOT THAT XMAS PACKAGE. IT WAS JUST WHAT I NEEDED, THANX.

CHAPTER 7

WAITING AND TRAINING

A month after the adrenalin-fueled Operation *Torch*, the Rangers' days consisted of training, playing poker, swimming, shooting the breeze, looking for French girls and yet more training. For a battalion of testosterone-fueled men who had signed up for nonstop action, days without any real fighting began to linger, moving more slowly than a tortoise crossing the Sahara.

At this point in the war, the British had recaptured Tobruk in Libya. The Germans and Russians continued fighting in Stalingrad, with the tides turning in the Soviet Army's favor when German forces retreated at Kotelnikovo. Meanwhile, in the Pacific General Douglas McArthur was leading the U.S. Army against the Japanese in New Guinea. Closer to home base, former Vichy leader French Admiral Darlan was assassinated in his headquarters in Algiers on December 24, Christmas Eve. During late December Colonel Darby was frequently AWOL and strange visitors began appearing at Headquarters. A sleek ship by the name of *Emma* would offer restless Rangers another chance at a night raid on a Mediterranean target. The British beauty was a tease. It would take another month before the men could participate in a history-making mission.

Phil's letter to his cousin Harriet brims with youthful innocence, like a letter home from camp.
When he told his mother he was a Ranger she thought he was putting out forest fires in England.
He kept up the ruse to shield her from worries.
PHIL STERN

***

NOVEMBER-DECEMBER 1942, ARZEW AND ORAN

Well, we're just about running the gamut in the type of money we get every payday. Just a couple of months ago we were receiving pound notes, shillings and ha' pennies. Now in Africa we get franc notes. The high denominations, like the 1,000 franc notes, are big babies, which we call "wall paper." The design on the note is quite elaborate with a picture of a native occupied at one of the North African industries (usually farming). The coloring is highly gaudy and the paper very cheap and thin. Seems as though every other franc note is patched with paper tape. Coins exist but are not too plentiful. It's always a surprise to me that these damn franc notes will actually buy things.

Immediately following payday the trek toward Oran gets started. Usually we go in small groups of about three and four. There's all sorts of things money can accomplish in Oran once you get started. Depends on your taste. Some guys just get stinko. Others want to merely look at the sights. Some search for female companionship. A sizable group makes a point of buying all sorts of souvenirs to send home to girlfriends, mothers, friends etc. Of course there's the I-love-life type of guy who runs down the line and gets his fill of all the above mentioned activities. But, brother, what a sad sack he turns out to be the following morning. An extremely sympathetic and understanding first sergeant is necessary for this glutton's welfare for the next few days. Come to think of it I could do with a bit more sleep myself.

It's pretty interesting to note the kind of items my franc notes will buy in a French Colonial city. I hereby appoint myself as an authority on this subject. At least three hundred of my hard-earned bucks have traveled to French and Arabian pocket books in the process of learning.

I have purchased woven raffia baskets, leather wallets, pocket books, cigarette boxes, carved animals, sandals, French art books (no, not the kinds you're thinking of!), paintings, rings, bracelets, leather pillow cases and an Arab fez. Shows you what a guy will do to impress people back home. And they're probably

Cemetery March: With future battles in mind, a company of Rangers keep in fighting shape with a speed march. Parallel to the road looms an old cemetery. "I was trying to be ironic and artistic with the soldiers marching in a row alongside the gravestones," said Stern. Unfortunately it would prove to be all too prophetic during costly later campaigns.
PHIL STERN

thinking that the poor boy must be suffering something awful in North Africa. The Red Cross Club bulletin board in Oran has a STARS AND STRIPES notice posted. It concerns the kind of souvenirs G.I.s are advised to buy.

Here is an excerpt:

> No doubts your first thoughts will turn to jewelry. There's plenty of it. Most of it is French and not African. Buying rings for their fingers puts bells on their toes. Don't buy a plain ring for a girl. Get something fancy with colored stones. If she's blond select the pastel colored stones. If she's brunette try a dark shade. If she's red headed give us the ring and her address.
> J.B. the gambling man

J.B. is a character and a definite legend in the First Ranger Battalion. J.B. stands for Jennings Bryan Coomer. He's really a

Colonel Darby leading the way out front returns from a long, grueling speed march with the
Rangers in the rugged mountains above Arzew.
PHIL STERN

very simple guy and perhaps it's unfair to call him things like
a "character" and a "legend." In civilian life J.B. lived in
Pampa, Texas. He did all sorts of work. He spent years as a
trouble-shooter on oil wells. He also has a flair for gambling
and ran a place in Texas. J.B. has an instinctive and thorough
understanding of the percentages and angles of any type of
gambling. His personal preference is stud poker and craps. Added
to all this J.B. has the most uncanny luck. He never loses.

The personnel boys who do the paper work on allotments and money
orders swear that J.B. sends home a minimum of one thousand bucks
a month. And he certainly doesn't earn this figure on his T-5
rating which nets him $79.20 each payday. J.B.'s army career

amounts to two and a half years at this point so it's a certainty that his wife is holding at least twenty thousand bucks for him. That's plenty of cabbage from any view point. And J.B. never has less than a thousand cold cash in his jeans. But there are some more important facts about J.B. which I'd like to relate. J.B. is warm, friendly and generally a nice guy. Just the opposite of what you'd expect of a Texas professional gambler. He'd never gamble with the battalion small fry. You know the kind of kid who plays a mild game planning not to lose over ten or fifteen bucks and never wins. J.B. would advise this guy not to gamble, and he would even take over the fellow's hand, win back the lost money plus an extra twenty. Give all the dough to the kid and have him walk off while the master would take over.

J.B. gambles and wins with the bigger boys, who have already taken away all the dough from the small fry. Whenever a Ranger is broke, J.B. wouldn't loan him dough, but give it to him. If a guy's wife at home has an operation coming up it's no surprise to see J.B. send off a hundred smackers to her. J.B. is definitely a big guy who makes a policy of watching over and protecting the little guy. He's only a Corporal and yet ends up with more money every month than Colonel Darby. And an overseas Colonel don't earn just pretzels. The Ranger officers always treat J.B. with great respect and tact. I don't know for sure but even officers have financial problems and J.B. certainly must be making the best of that situation.

* * *

Our training period is about over. We're ready for something big. It's not official and Colonel Darby hasn't taken me into his confidence to let me know the lowdown. But we all know it, feel it. There's something in the air. Even the Arzew sand dunes sort of whisper it. It's a hard thing to explain. Maybe it's because a military group develops a sensitivity as though we are molded into a compact gang of guys, all the same ideas and thoughts. The battalion pace is already changed. Everybody is definitely high strung, anxious, questioning. First sergeants looking harried, officers stop kidding with the men. Strange visitors begin to appear at battalion headquarters. G.I. artillery officers, British commando representatives, some naval guys, and even a few French officers.

ABOVE No snowflakes fell in Arzew on Christmas Day, 1942. Instead Rangers stood under the rays of the hot sun on Red Beach for religious services conducted by Father Basil. Sergeant Crandall played music on a small portable organ that Basil had managed to secure. Carols and hymns were sung by the rough and tough Rangers in celebration of the holiday.

PHIL STERN

LEFT An enterprising Arabian boy named Achmed marches in step with a Browning Automatic Rifle slung across his back. With a fondness for "chawcalott" rations, he made a deal with Rangers to carry their gear when they'd reached their limit during exhausting speed marches, in exchange for chocolate.

PHIL STERN

NEXT PAGES With the majority of young men away from home for the first time, a makeshift Christmas tree adds a bit of tradition and comfort to the holiday celebration.

PHIL STERN

Nobody sees Colonel Darby much lately. When he's not in conference the old boy takes off on some mysterious trip. One of his junkets lasts about four days. Word spreads around that he's on a submarine doing some reconnaissance off Sicily. Some say it's Sardinia. Frankly, I don't know just what these trips represent. Anybody's guess is as good as mine. But some day when the war is over, if both of us live through it, I'm going to say, "Bill, for God's sake tell me. Did you really go on a submarine ride to Sicily?"

J.B. has been spending lots of time at headquarters of late. And he's particularly close to some of the big boys. They're smoking J.B.'s imported cigars together. Between puffs, there's some pretty intimate conversation. J.B. has that look on his puss. He knows something, hell of a lot too.

"What's cooking J.B.?" I ask him. "Oh nothing, baby," he says. "I know you better than that J.B., come clean huh?" It's like pulling teeth but J.B. gets very ceremonious. Quietly pulls me over to the motorcycle hut. He glances around nervously and says, "Kid, something is up. And it ain't chicken feed." I wish he'd tell me more, damn him. And he does. J.B. just can't help thinking along the lines of a gambler.

He says, "Phil, this is a deal where both sides have loaded dice. The winner will be the guy who discovers the 'load' first and acts fast." My eyes and ears are popping. Why in hell doesn't this Texas Ranger shoot it to me straight from the shoulder? And J.B. is one Southerner who doesn't drawl over his sentences. He talks with a fast, nervous clip and when he's really excited J.B. will stammer just slightly. "We're going to hit inland installations this time and there ain't any Frenchies there. This time it's the Axis. Jerries and Macaronis. There's no aces up our sleeve either. We gotta outplay them from the deck." Now we're getting some place. "But," I ask J.B., "don't you know where we're heading? Is it in Africa, France, Italy, Sicily or Brooklyn? We going by ship, air or train?" J.B. isn't saying anymore. "Just wait and watch," he advises. I don't doubt J.B.'s words. He always has the inside dope. So I'll wait and watch.

If I have even the slightest doubt about J.B.'s veracity, it is dispelled in very short order. It just takes three days after J.B. gives me the dope to receive official confirmation. The guy must be hexed or something. Arzew Beach suddenly gets all a flutter due to a new moving order handed out by all company commanders.

Someone can easily suspect that old J.B. must have contact with Roosevelt and Churchill too. This time every man is to carry just his bedroll, field pack and weapon. Extra socks, underwear and stuff go into the bedroll. All barracks bags to remain at the bivouac area. That means we will come back. Eventually.

PRINCESS EMMA

December 26, 1942. Arzew harbor, Algeria

We have a repeat of Corker Hill in Scotland. We form by companies and this time we march. No trucks. The hike is up the beach on to the Arzew highway. We call it Highway 66. Our destination is the docks. On the way we sing songs. I wish I could repeat them but the boys carefully note familiar landmarks as we pass by: the Brasserie, the lady who does our laundry, Arzew City Hall with the Mayor peeking out at us. We even greet Arzew's mutts. By this time we know every dog in Arzew by his first name. They bark and wag their tails and join in on the march. And the little kids join in too. Matters begin to get a bit confusing for platoon sergeants who are trying to keep the hike orderly. Even Achmed shows up. He suspects the worst and raises hell with us. Achmed built up a very lucrative gun-toting business and he resents our leaving.

Yes sir, it's a boat ride. Lying out in Arzew harbor is one of the sleekest, neatest, little ships I've ever seen. Right at the stone jetties awaiting us are about a dozen British manned landing craft. The same babies that ferried us on to the beaches of North Africa, November 8th, 1942. We proceed. It's a beach landing in reverse. Now the landing boats putter to the ship. The Mediterranean waters are smooth and friendly today. And we don't have to duck

NEXT PAGES Aboard the modern, sleek *Princess Emma*, Rangers gather around to get the dope from Colonel Darby about a top-secret mission. It would be another night attack, this time on the island of La Galite, northwest of Bizerte. The plan was to hit the beach, blow up a radio station that was hindering air operations in the Mediterranean, knock out a garrison and take prisoners. The operation was aborted, much to the Rangers' dismay.
PHIL STERN

1st Ranger Battalion's F Company officers Lieutenant Walter F. Nye, Lieutenant Leilyn Young and
Captain Roy Murray aboard H.M.S. *Princess Emma* in Arzew harbor, December 1942. After the
Tunisian campaign, they served with the 4th Ranger Battalion during the invasion of Sicily.
PHIL STERN

below as we ply through the waters to the ship. Seagulls keep
flying all around us. They don't look any different than the gulls
at the Brooklyn Navy Yard. The town of Arzew seems to draw away
into the hills for protection. We can still see its natives
milling around the dock area watching us float away. I begin to
realize we've been something quite new and exciting in their
lives. They're a swell people come to think of it.

The bow of our new ship seems proud of its name. In blue grey
letters we can read H.M.S. PRINCESS EMMA. Boarding the PRINCESS
is an experience members of the First Ranger Battalion will

remember for many years. No climbing up ropes here. Elaborate motor driven pulleys pull the entire landing craft up to deck level and we simply walk off, like gentlemen. His Majesty's ship is some deal: modern to the ninth degree. She is clean, neat and powerful and has enough fire power to blow a whole navy. We can't get over it. Our last ship was a rust bucket in comparison. PRINCESS EMMA is no shy gal either. She's paid surprise visits to the coast of France and Norway where her gun-toting passengers have knocked the hell out of Axis emplacements and scrammed. The crew boys tell us all sorts of hair-raising exploits in which their "EMMA" participated.

J.B. just walks around the ship, beaming and looking generally very happy. You've got to hand it to that guy. Yes, PRINCESS EMMA is our sweetheart now and we look forward to some damn interesting trips with her. Colonel Darby is in great spirits too. He spends a bit of time with the skipper but mainly he's tied up with executive officers and company commanders. We all expect important news shortly. Darby stops to talk with anxious privates, explaining that after a few more staff meetings he'll let the cat out of the bag. In the meantime some guys starts spreading the rumor that the First Ranger Battalion is heading back for the States where we're wanted to goose step down Broadway. Colonel Darby scratches that stuff soon enough.

We're on the PRINCESS EMMA but three days when a big informal gathering is ordered on the forward gun deck. Standing on the very nose of PRINCESS EMMA is Colonel Darby. He faces aft. In front of Wild Bill is the whole battalion. The men are so compact they don't occupy much space. Some of the guys are even hanging down from the six-inch guns. It's a sunny afternoon and any schoolteacher would give a million bucks for the attention Darby is getting now. As usual, we get the dope from our Colonel, short and sweet. He gives us the general idea to be followed by details from company commanders and platoon sergeants. This is what the whole deal boils down to: an island named La Galite near Bizerte, in the straits of Sicily, a radio station, a little town and a ship out in the harbor. We're to hit the beaches at night, head for an inland radio station and blow it up, make for town to knock out an enemy garrison and take some prisoners. Simultaneously with this action, a special squad will board a docked ship and try to capture her intact. Otherwise blow her up. Denny Bergstrom

is in on this deal and he starts looking around for guys to whom he owes dough to pay up. Some of the boys who bet that we'd sail to the U.S. pay through the nose now. They pay reluctantly and admit it was all wishful thinking.

Blam! It's like when you're in love with a girl and she bats you down. That's what happens with PRINCESS EMMA and us. I don't even care to talk about it. Nobody does. What a buildup we get. What a beautiful set of battle plans Darby hands us! And then blooey! The whole she-bang is called off at the PRINCESS EMMA. There is no talk and the mood is ugly. PRINCESS EMMA turns out to be a phony sweetheart. Frankly, I can't remember a thing about our march back to Arzew Beach. I know that I'm a sad, disappointed kid with lots of company. Kids and dogs might have followed us back, if so I don't recall it. Arzew itself might have had an earthquake but I couldn't even vouch for that. The days that follow are just a hazy recollection of brooding.

Things can't be lousy all the time and because of new orders we soon snap out of it. This time the camp is alerted. All passes canceled. And every man must be prepared for moving at one hour's notice. This ought to make up for that damn PRINCESS EMMA. Anyway we've got some new hope. The boys begin to become themselves again.

ABOVE LEFT Sergeant John Ingram pushes his buddy Private First Class Robert Lowell in an ammunition cart. All the men pictured were in the best shape of their lives. Well-liked for his dynamic personality, Ingram was mortally wounded during the bitter fighting in Venafro, Italy, in 1943.
PHIL STERN

LEFT A few games of baseball help soothe the Rangers' disappointment about the scrapped operation and the luxury accommodations on H.M.S. *Princess Emma.* By this time the men were chomping at the bit for another night raid.
PHIL STERN

CHAPTER 8

NICKEL BEER AND FREE LOVE

Still sulking in the aftermath of the scrapped raid on H.M.S. *Princess Emma*, the brooding Rangers returned to Arzew. A few weeks later they were assigned to the Fifth Army Invasion Training Center, where they would demonstrate their expertise with live fire and amphibious landing techniques. On February 1, a caravan of trucks rumbled down the road carrying new replacements to bolster the ranks. A total of 100 men and six officers fresh from the States were given a rousing Ranger welcome replete with grenades and live hot bullets. Phil was summoned by Darby to pack up for a top-secret mission aboard a C-47 carrying an eccentric cast of characters that included a World War I pigeon wrangler and his pigeon, an airsick Stars and Stripes reporter and the nonstop chatterbox, Captain Saam. They were in for a bumpy ride.

***

FEBRUARY 1, 1943: IN THE SKIES ABOVE TUNISIA

"Wild Bill wants ya right away kiddo, and make it snappy." That's how Tony Rada greets me. Before I can ask what's up, Tony

---

Darby, Phil and Captain Saam, the demolition man, take a top-secret ride on a C-47 transport aircraft from La Senia Airport to Maison Blanche Airport in Algiers.
PHIL STERN

151

disappears down the beach. Wonder what Darby wants me for? I find out soon enough. At headquarters the Colonel says, "Stern, can you pack up your bedroll, field pack, cameras and a good film supply in fifteen minutes?"

I tell him "Yep." That's another faux pas for me. "By God, Stern, you'll never make a soldier. Anyway you have the distinction of being about the only man here who can lean so sloppily on the table and say 'Yep!' and get away with it!"

"Sorry Sir," I say. There Darby goes, getting prolific again. "If you're ready in fifteen minutes you're in for a nice plane ride. So hop to it."

For a free plane ride I can pack a movie queen's wardrobe in fifteen minutes. So this detail is pretty easy. J.B. walks in and offers to help me. "What in hell are we up to now?" I ask J.B. As usual J.B. has the answer at his fingertip. "You're going with the advance party," he explains. "There'll be five of you: Colonel Darby, Captain Saam, Tony Rada, Johnny Rembecki and yourself, baby." J.B. ends up saying that he's going to drive us all out to La Senia Airport in Colonel Darby's jeep. I wait until everyone piles into the jeep so that I can get a photo taken. Who knows? This jeep ride might be the beginning of a terrific future. But Colonel Darby is quite impatient and says, "Don't you know there's a war on, son? Sometimes, Stern, I think that in the brain area of your skull there is lodged a roll of panchromatic film."

So I climb in and J.B. steps on the gas. It's funny about these jeeps. Colonel Darby is sitting up front, I'm directly behind. I'm tall and my feet are sprawled up against the back of Darby's seat. I forget that the seats have an open space where a guy sits. Colonel Darby swings his head around at me and says, "Stern, will you please stop goosing me."

The ride to La Senia Airport is uneventful. The airport looks pretty much like any other airdrome. Off to one side is a graveyard for a bunch of old broken down French planes. The field itself is humming with activity. Mostly transport planes and a few fighters. Colonel Darby goes into Base Operations and comes out accompanied by an Air Corps Major and Lieutenant.

All of us then head for a C-47 whose engines are aboard, leaving J.B. outside in his jeep. With no adieu at all, our plane taxis down the field to the concrete runway. J.B. waves his arms until we don't see him anymore.

You can't beat traveling by plane. It's smooth, comfortable and fast. These Army transports are the same as the commercial lines back home. Except that the G.I. plane doesn't have all the fancy insides. No stewardess either. Our seats are made of aluminum and are hinged to the side of the plane. For a while I just squint my eyes to look out at the terrain below. Oran is a big city and after passing it we come upon farmland and mountains. That's all we see between cities. Colonel Darby takes a little snooze. Captain Saam and I start talking about different things. First he tells me that we'll be in Algiers tonight and that he and Colonel Darby have some businesses at Allied Head Quarters (HQ) in there. Then Captain Saam tells me about his background as an engineer for the coalmines in Pennsylvania. His job was to blast certain parts of the mine with TNT and dynamite. "You see, Phil, I've been blowing things up since childhood. I love to see explosions and blow things up. That's why I'm the demolitions officer of the First Ranger Battalion." And Captain Saam ain't kidding.

Colonel Darby is still snoozing. Tony Rada and Johnny Rembecki doze off. Captain Saam and I continue gabbing. Saam has a long, red mustache which curls up at both ends. He takes meticulous care of the thing as though he were in a mustache contest and a block of dynamite is the prize. At first I used to get a little nervous talking to Saam because when he answered, his mustache would wiggle up and down with the movements of his lips. But I'm used to it now and it doesn't affect me at all.

For some reason we suddenly talk about insurance. Saam says that he's not taking any chances. So he has himself completely covered by G.I. and civilian insurance. I explain that I have a funny feeling about insurance. I figure if I have 10,000 bucks-worth of insurance I will certainly get killed in this war. I admit this idea has no scientific basis at all. It's just a hunch of mine, which I intend to follow through like a Holy Roller. Of course if I had a wife and kids I certainly would get insurance in simple consideration for my dependants. The way it stands if I were to be knocked off and my mother got 10,000 bucks, I know damn well she'd get a blood hemorrhage every time she spent a nickel of it. I wouldn't wish such a fate to anyone. So I don't take any insurance. Captain Saam's mustache wiggles a bit in confusion. He says I take a rather unique attitude.

"Very interesting," he says. "Very interesting." In order not to confuse my Captain any further I decide not to tell him that I also make a point of squandering most of my money and lose the rest at craps. I do this because I don't want to have any dough accumulated. My hunch is that I'd never survive to enjoy it. I even wrote home for the folks to sell my car and use the money for furniture.

The plane's speed is suddenly cut down. We begin to lose altitude. From the Plexiglas windows we can see Algiers. We circle around the airport awhile to make way for other traffic. The landing is smooth. Only bumpy part is when we taxi up to the Base Operations Building. The Algiers Airport is called "Maison Blanche," by the French. It means white house. This airfield is far bigger than La Senia and the traffic is like Times Square. Over here there's transports, fighters, bombers and French commercial planes as Algiers is Allied Headquarters.

Tony, Johnny and I go over to the transient barracks. Colonel Darby gives us instructions to remain at the barracks while he and Captain Saam go to Allied HQ. They will return in the morning and we'll all take off again. This must really be important because the same plane and its crew are at the Colonel's disposal. Darby also tells us that we'll be informed about where we're going and why when we hit our next airport.

The plane ride gets all the boys pretty tired and after chow we spread out our bedrolls on the granite floor and fall asleep in a hurry. When you're good and tired, a granite floor and three blankets are quite comfy. The only reason we wake up during the night is that some Jerry planes come over and drop a few eggs far to the outside of the airdrome. The anti-aircraft batteries let loose until Jerry decides he isn't welcome and flies away. We're all satisfied about the bad marksmanship and go to sleep again.

Colonel Darby and Captain Saam return to Maison Blanche airport quite chipper and generally happy about things. I'd give anything to know what happened at Allied Headquarters. "Let's shove off, men," says the Colonel. And we walk briskly toward the YARDBIRD, our plane. For some reason an airport is always windy even if it's perfectly calm everywhere else. So all of us, the pilots, Tony, Johnny and myself, Colonel Darby and Captain Saam must battle the wind to reach our transport.

TOP In addition to his curlicued red mustache, Captain Frederick "Sammy" Saam was obsessed with demolitions, most likely due to his previous job as an engineer in a Pennsylvania coal mine, where part of his job involved blasting the mines with TNT.
PHIL STERN

ABOVE After a night in the barracks at Maison Blanche, the men board the *Yardbird*, a C-47 transport aircraft heading to Youks-les-Bains airfield in Algeria. A couple of eccentric passengers join the ride: a World War I pigeon wrangler and an airsick rookie reporter named Ralph Martin, who later became Phil's coworker at *Stars and Stripes*.
PHIL STERN

Saam has a tough time controlling his big red mustache, which insists on blowing around his face and ears. And out of the corner of my eye I can see Colonel Darby nervously glancing at Saam's temperamental lip gear.

Looks like we have a couple of hitchhikers sitting around next to YARDBIRD. There's a short stocky Lieutenant leaning on some wicker crates and a thin, lanky kid sitting on his bedroll. The pilot has a talk with them and then consults Darby. Colonel Darby nods his head, which means we have two more passengers. Personally I don't mind. I'm a bit tired of talking about TNT blocks and insurance with Captain Saam. It'll be okay by me to have some new guys to talk to on the second lap of our trip.

Again, the takeoff is neat and smooth showing that our pilot really knows his onions. I keep looking at these two new characters and wonder what their angle is. About thirty minutes out of Maison Blanche we all get acquainted. The Lieutenant is Wendell Stratton and those wicker crates contain a platoon of Signal Corps pigeons, which are under his command. He's taking the birds up to the front. The long legged kid is Sergeant Ralph Martin, who is the front line reporter for STARS AND STRIPES, the soldiers' newspaper. I can hardly see the pigeons through the thick baskets but I can hear them cooing. Colonel Darby develops a sudden interest in pigeons and he goes over to the baskets, opens one, and pets the bird. I can't exactly make out my Colonel's remarks but it's something like "ootchy kootchy koo." He's a great guy, my Colonel. He makes friends with the pigeon Lieutenant and asks a lot of questions about these birds. Sergeant Martin rips open his bedroll and pulls out a big pad of paper and busts in on the Colonel, saying, "Do you mind if I ask some questions too? These pigeons will make a swell yarn for STARS AND STRIPES."

So the poor pigeon guy gets a million questions fired at him. Darby wants to know what they eat. The Lieutenant says, "Oh they're the biggest chow hounds in the world. They weigh about sixteen ounces and eat their own weight in food every week. We feed them small corn, green peas, wheat, oats, canary seed and cod liver oil."

Sergeant Martin, his pencil doing acrobatics on the pad, asks, "How does the Army get the birds, Lieutenant?" The pigeon officer has the answers right off the bat.

"Why, our pigeons are draftees just like everybody else. In civilian life they weren't just ordinary birds. They earned all sorts of cups and trophies for being well trained. Came the war and the Signal Corps requisitioned them for special combat training."

Even Captain Saam wants to know all about the G.I. pigeons. His mustache jiggles about during the discussion. The Lieutenant himself is very delighted to be the center of all this interest. He's been a pigeon fancier all his life. He loves pigeons. He knows all their habits, problems and history. That's his meat. Nothing can hold Lieutenant Stratton back now. So he expands further, along historical lines.

"In the First World War," he points out, "our doughboys captured a German pigeon by the name of Kaiser, and have since then bred some of the U.S. Army's finest pigeons. Most pigeons live to about twelve or fourteen years. But Kaiser is one exception. Right now he is twenty-three years old and living off a fat pension back in the States."

By this time even the co-pilot leaves his controls to get a lie on the Signal Corps birds. He insists that with so many pigeons around, Lieutenant Stratton's men must certainly never suffer from lack of food. After the dirty look from Stratton, the Air Corps guy wobbles back to his controls.

Boy what a scene this damn plane makes. With everybody from the Colonel down to the buck private, all hypnotized by Lieutenant Stratton's talk about the pigeons. I wonder what the pigeons are thinking of? Probably cod liver oil. We can't stop the birds' commanding officer now.

"In the last war, the Sergeant York of the pigeons was Cher Ami, who saved the Lost Battalion by bringing an S.O.S message to Allied HQ. Cher Ami flew through heavy fire, had his leg shot off and held the message by his tendons alone. Similar pigeons are now carried on bombers raiding Germany, just in case. On several occasions these birds fly back to England with the news of a bomber's crashing and other valuable intelligence. And for your information," he continues, "Pigeons have great intelligence. On the boat coming over to Africa we built two pigeon coops on the ship's bridge. Six of the birds apparently didn't like their overseas assignment and they flew all the way back to the States where I'm informed all six are being held by the MPs for desertion.

I don't know if Army regulations says anything about court martials for pigeons."

At this point, I'm sorry to say, the STARS AND STRIPES reporter is turning green and purple and looks very sick. Colonel Darby asks, "What's wrong, son?"

"Guess I'm airsick, Sir," Sergeant Martin says. "Ridiculous," Darby tells him. "It's all a matter of the mind. All you have to do is relax. Now wiggle your toes. Now wiggle your elbows in synchronization with your toes. That'll take care of you, my boy." Following Darby's advice makes the reporter look like a monkey. So as Sergeant Martin makes with the wiggles, Lieutenant Stratton proceeds to inform us about the pigeons' love life.

"You must understand," he says, "that pigeons have a family life just like humans. And the pigeon who flies the fastest to deliver his message and get back again is the one who has been separated from his mate on their wedding night. And the Signal Corps is very understanding beyond the mere confines of communications."

This pigeon business is getting better and better all the time. Even Sergeant Martin forgets all about his airsickness.

Because of the various distractions aboard the YARDBIRD, I fail to note that we have two Spitfires as escorts. They fly so fast that they must travel in circles in order to stay with us. Also, it's no secret now that we're flying over Tunisia and the Spitfires show that German air patrols must be zooming around this area. It's a relief to land at Youks-les-Bains Airfield, a barren looking place in the middle of a desert. There are no buildings or towers here just dug-outs and foxholes. Surrounding the field I can see British anti-aircraft crews united with their 40mm Bofors pointing into the sky. Pretty desolate looking but it feels a little better than being up in the air with German patrol planes after us.

Our two hitchhikers with their pigeons and notebooks finally leave us. Our party goes one way and they take off in another direction. Colonel Darby waves thanks to the YARDBIRD crew for a swell ride and we head for Base Operations, which is merely a big hole dug into a hill at the side of the airport. Darby spends only five minutes there and calls us to get chow. The Youks-les-Bains Airfield mess line is very simple yet democratic. It's an outdoor mess serving C-ration meat and beans, G.I. coffee and hard tack. Nothing more. No bucking of the line. Everybody stands in line waiting his turn. Colonels, majors, captains, buck privates and even second looeys are social equals at this meal. I feel pretty important getting my mess gear filled with meat and beans and Colonel Darby waiting behind me for his share. The boys back in Camp Crowder would love to see me now.

We're a cozy little group. Sitting around on rocks and crates. Thanks to the Air Corps mess sergeant, our C-rations are prepared so it tastes very good. And that's a real accomplishment.

While drinking our coffee Colonel Darby has us all draw closer and he does the talking. "Lads," he says, "This is it. Youks-les-Bains is but seventeen miles from Tébessa, the gigantic Allied Supply Dump. Rommel's Panzers are about forty miles from the supply dump." The Colonel looks at his wristwatch and continues. "In two hours our battalion will land right here in thirty-three transport planes. The only ones to remain at Arzew are the supply, kitchen and personnel boys. They will start out by trucks in a few days and join us. And before long we'll be contacting Fritz and his Macaroni friends. After that, if we do well, perhaps we'll all get back to nickel beer and free love."

Nickel Beer and Free Love. That's an expression Colonel Darby uses very often. He never tells anyone exactly what he means by it. I suppose everybody gets a different meaning of the phrase. I figure it this way: It's a phrase, slogan or battle cry meaning cheap drinks and plenty of gals but there is really a deeper meaning. The Colonel uses the expression when he refers to the good times the battalion had in the past like the period in Scotland when we had a three-week furlough in civilian billets. He also uses the term to represent better times ahead.

I guess Nickel Beer and Free Love shows Colonel Darby's desire to fight hard, help get the war over with, and finally "March down Broadway." And he's got an entire battalion with just that idea in their collective noodle.

CHAPTER 9

TÉBESSA

EARLY FEBRUARY 1943

It isn't very often that an entire battalion of infantrymen is flown over seven hundred miles to the front. It's a great thrill to watch a formation of thirty-three transport planes hit the steel runway one by one. And in every one of those ships there's buddies of mine. Takes about an hour for all the planes to land and taxi off the runways. The boys pour out laughing and raising hell generally. The mortar squads roll out of the planes with their carts and ammo. The rifleman, machine gunners and officers touch their feet to the ground again and feel at home. Colonel Darby scampers around to all companies, greeting them and checking up on personnel.

From nowhere, it seems, a whole lineup of two and a half ton trucks show up on the highway next to the airfield. They're ours. And it doesn't take long for the entire battalion to occupy the vehicles. These trucks are driven by Negro boys from the Quartermaster Depot. They're a strong, brawny bunch of guys and seem well fit for their nerve-wrecking jobs. These boys spend all their time driving troops and ammunition to the front, mostly at night which means no lights and the constant chance of dropping down a ditch or hitting mines placed by enemy patrols. The drivers are very friendly and tell us about their experience

Darby and liaison officers of the U.S. Army Air Force discuss enemy concentrations in the nearby hills. Ranger radio patrols working within the enemy lines kept constant contact with the Air Force, directing strafing and bombing sorties from the ground. Dernaia Pass, Tunisia, 1943.
PHIL STERN

in the last few days. I'll stick to the infantry. These damn trucks make too big a target.

The First Ranger Battalion has been pretty lucky so far. And what a lucky break we have by leaving the airport when we do. Just as the last truck of C Company pulls out of Youks-les-Bains Airfield, Jerry bombers start plastering the joint. The planes are so high up all we can see are little specks. A few moments later the air-raid siren goes off. Whining like hell. That's a nice how-do-you-do. Out here they have the air raid first, then the air-raid alarm. Boy, do our drivers step on the gas. I never saw a two and a half ton truck travel so fast. And what a racket develops. The truck engine groaning like all hell, the bomb hits going "whop whop" and the 40mm Bofors sounding like pom pom pom pom pom. Now I know why we call the British anti-aircraft guns Pom Poms.

This little deal lasts just a matter of a couple of minutes. Before we know it, the Jerry planes are gone. But the pom poms keep blasting the sky. We're a lucky bunch of boys that Jerry didn't come over with fighters. Then we'd really be duck soup for strafing. Our trucks beat down the road toward Tébessa and each vehicle rides about two hundred yards from the next one. This is considered proper dispersal in case of air attack.

As we get closer to Tébessa I notice piles of crates and boxes off the side of the road. A little while more and the roadside gets even more cluttered up. I can see row upon row of 105mm and 155mm shells. In another area there's all sorts of wire spools and other Signal Corps equipment, plenty of cases of small-caliber ammunition, food supplies, gas and oil drums.

Under camouflage nets the engineers have their bulldozers, caterpillar tractors and other paraphernalia. This stuff repeats itself and extends for a lot of miles. I now catch on to what Colonel Darby means by "Tébessa: the Gigantic Allied Supply Dump." Seeing all this gear certainly boosts a guy's morale.

The town of Tébessa looks the same as any other French North African city. There are a few different things though. In this town they have a gang of ancient Roman ruins. Looks like a picture out of my public school history book. The tall granite columns are still standing although the walls and ceilings are mostly crumbled down. We find these old broken down buildings on the same streets which have the houses of today.

The people in Tébessa go wild when they watch American soldiers rumble through their streets. They're a bit more excited about us here than in Oran or Arzew. The Germans are closer by and how they hate the Jerries. Just mention "Boche" (German soldier) to any of these people and see what happens. They'll rattle off a lot of nasty sounding French and finish with a strong pair of thumbs pointed down. I also notice some white walls with "Vive Pétain" printed on them but the Pétain is crossed out and de Gaulle is painted over it. The kids seem the same as all over. They're not worried much over French politics. The petite Frenchmen are all over the streets playing marbles. Their game is different than ours. These kids use round stones instead of glass agates and they don't shoot the stones with their fingers, they throw the stuff underhanded. Some kids romp through the ancient Roman ruins. I guess they're more educated.

Fortunately there is a beautiful wooded area outside of Tébessa on the side of a big mountain. It looks like almost any forest in upstate New York. Lots of trees, shrubbery growing out of a series of little hills. The mountain is tremendous and can be seen from any part of the area. The natural protection is made to order. We couldn't ask for a better bivouac area. This place marks the end of our truck ride from Youks-les-Bains Airfield. Anyway, this is the first lap of our trip to the front lines.

We set up camp here and we look like a gang of Robin Hoods in Sherwood Forest with Oneskunk as Friar Tuck. Only difference is that we're loaded to the teeth with rifles, Tommy guns, machine guns and mortars. There isn't a bow and arrow within a thousand miles. We set up our pup tents and prepare to wait for further orders. Each man carries a shelter-half in his pack. The shelter-half is an odd shaped chunk of canvas with buttons. Two guys pool their shelter-halves and after a little acrobatics, we have a pup tent. The same two guys are partners now and bunk in the pup tent. The mattress consists of Mother Earth and as many blankets we can drum up. All equipment and personal stuff is stored therein. For guys over six feet tall, pup tents are annoying. This is because the guy's body lives in one climate and his feet in another. Luckily, I'm only five feet eleven inches with my G.I. shoes on.

Not much happens while we wait for orders at Tébessa. It's a healthy, outdoor life though and we spend lots of time going over all our equipment. All weapons are stripped and the parts cleaned thoroughly. We check on all our ammunition, make sure there's no corrosion. Chow is served by kitchen trucks, supplied by the Second Army Corps. The battalion contributes men for the Kitchen Patrol details. Colonel Darby isn't around much. He's got business at Second Corps Headquarters. This HQ is an unusual one. It's like a big apartment drilled into the side of the Tébessa Mountains. I understand G.I. engineers worked on this project for weeks.

Our life in "Sherwood Forest" lasts only three days. We're on the move and it's two and a half ton trucks again. This time we must travel by night because Jerry isn't far away now. We start out late in the afternoon just as it starts to get dark. The trucks have been sheltered under large trees. I'm assigned to the truck carrying Headquarters Company. Denny Bergstrom and Tony Rada are in the same group. We drive down the dirt road toward the highway. Nights get very cold out here. And I don't have an overcoat. I figure riding in an open truck at night without a coat won't be so hot. Now to cook up a coat.

Right near the highway there is a very unusual supply dump. It's a big tent with all sorts of equipment inside. About five guys handle the deal. G.I.s who don't appreciate Army red tape enjoy this new supply system. "Hey, you guys got any extra G.I. coats?" I holler at them. They don't answer but some little half pint guy throws a brand new coat up into the truck so that it practically knocks me over. Other Rangers holler for gloves, woolen caps and socks. The stuff just gets thrown at the boys. No statements are signed, no records, no nothing. As we pull out off the dirt road, the supply guys yell, "Good luck fellas, beat

ABOVE RIGHT After two days of flying and eight hours of riding in an open truck, Phil landed in Gafsa, which he described as like a chapter from *National Geographic*. Early one morning he woke to see a procession of camels and Arab families packed up with mattresses, pots and pans, probably heading for the rear areas.
PHIL STERN

RIGHT Taking a chance loading up a jeep filled with important bigwigs, Phil joins Colonel Darby and a cadre of Ranger officers as they conduct reconnaissance ahead of a planned raid in Gafsa, in February 1943. Passengers included Major Herman Dammer, Major Alvah Miller, First Lieutenant Leonard Dirkes, Captain Roy Murray and Lieutenant Colonel Max Schneider.
PHIL STERN

the hell out of those Nazi bastards."

By the time we really get under way, it's dark. As we drive past the Tébessa Mountains the terrain gets more and more desolate. We're on flat landscape now and it's hard to see much detail. Every once in a while we can see a bonfire set up by the Air Corps to guide their planes at night. They call this highway Stuka Alley because Jerry planes make frequent visits to annoy American supply lines. This is no fairy tale because in the fields along Stuka Alley, I can detect hulks of planes, trucks and I notice one tank. Too dark to figure out what side they belong to. Anyway we're riding in open trucks and every guy knows just what spot he's going to jump from in case any planes come our way.

After several hours of riding, we reach the town of Fériana. This burg is a weird looking place, like a dead city. There are buildings, streets, stores but no lights at all and no people. The only sounds are churning motors and the MP traffic station guys, who yell out direction orders. There's a traffic jam here and the poor MPs have one hell of a time straightening things out. On motorcycles they race up and down the road eliminating snags. On one street corner I can make out a photographic shop with the shutters down and a big sign with the Leica trademark. I guess I really can smell a photographic shop at any distance.

Stuka Alley extends through Fériana toward Gafsa. And that's where we're heading for, Gafsa. Same road, same scenery, same riding as we've had from Tébessa to Fériana. Although the closer we get to Gafsa the more vegetation appears. The outskirts of town are lousy with palm trees. The black shapes of these trees show clearly against the night sky. We bypass Gafsa and end up in a suburb where there are a few long shallow buildings with big round domes in the center. The buildings are chalk white, making them easy to see in the dark night.

At one point our trucks swerve off the road into a sandy path, which leads into what seems like a forest. This is damn queer terrain, lots of sand and trees. Have to wait until morning to figure it out. It's tough for the trucks to make it through the sand. But these are powerful babies and after watching them churn through this sand, I believe they could climb up the side of a mountain. The line of trucks halt a very short distance down the line. There are trees nearby. Company commanders bark out orders to bivouac here for the night. A tired bunch of guys climb out of the trucks. Over eight hours riding open trucks gets you tired. And the bitter cold don't help too much. Some of the more enterprising kids set up pup tents. But most of the guys tear open their bedrolls, arrange the blankets into a sort of bag and crawl in. The sand makes a good mattress and forms into an indentation of the same shape as your body. Sleep comes easy.

Gafsa is like a chapter from NATIONAL GEOGRAPHIC. The morning after our tour through Stuka Alley we rub our eyes. The strong morning sunlight makes us blink a bit. The first thing we see is a procession of camels and Arabs. They must be heading for the rear areas. The camels are packed down with mattresses, pots and pans, kids, pet dogs and the men. These Arabs do things a little different. The woman of the family walks and carries additional paraphernalia on her back. And she don't look too happy about it. In the distance are the chalky white buildings with the domes in the center. These are the Arab mosques. Early in the morning some Arab gets into the dome and prays to the heavens. The guy who prays gets very shrill and loud as he gets along. His voice carries for miles when it's good and quiet and the wind is blowing right. Allah is the Arab's God and though it's weird to us, we can't kick. The GUIDE TO NORTH AFRICA said things would be strange here.

Gafsa happens to be a great date-growing sector, hence all the palm trees. There's dates all over the place. All you have to do is reach for them. If that's too tough, a bar of G.I. soap will get you a barrel full. At first dates taste okay. After a while they get on your nerves and if you don't see any again, it's a pleasure. It's at this point that the rest of the personnel section of the battalion arrives from Arzew by truck. Which also means that back mail catches up with us. I am very happy because the mail orderly hands me batches of mail and two lusty packages. The letters are okay but my West Coast pals and my mother hit upon the simultaneous idea of sending me big cartons of California dates. War has its hardships.

The Ranger cooks, supply men and personnel boys finally show up at Gafsa after their long motor trip from Arzew. They claim to have crossed over a dozen mountains, hit blizzards in the high country and stayed in the best French hotels overnight. With this section of the battalion back in Gafsa, we go to town to set up house. We take over an abandoned schoolhouse for headquarters with all companies bivouacked nearby. Pup tents get set up in the schoolyard. Convenient foxholes are dug right next to the tent. The kitchen truck establishes business on the side road near the schoolhouse. HQ and personnel take over the schoolhouse.

J.B. turns out to be my pup tent partner. Between the both of us we put together one of the best tents in the battalion. Under the blankets we stuff a lot of Gafsa straw. Some wooden boxes make a combination of shelves and tables for our personal stuff. J.B. drums up a big G.I. flash lamp which serves for our reading and writing lamp. From my barracks bag I dig up some eight by ten inch photos of Betty Grable and Ann Sheridan. These items make the decorations. Now we're fortified. Come what may.

Captain Bill Martin takes a jeep and three men to do some reconnaissance outside of Gafsa. There are a lot of Italian outposts toward the east and that's the direction Captain Martin and his men take for their jeep ride. Captain Saam, the demolition man, is a bit jealous and demands that he be sent on the next reconnaissance detail. Who knows? There might be something or other to blow up.

A muddy, beaten up old jeep comes tear-assing into the schoolyard the next morning. Just as muddy and beaten up is the driver. He climbs out and walks over toward us. It's the STARS AND STRIPES guy, Sergeant Ralph Martin, who left us at Youks-les-Bains. "Hi Rangers," he says. "Boy, I've been chasing around all last night and this morning trying to find you guys. Anyway I've caught up. I'm going to hang around until I can write a good yarn on the Rangers." Sergeant Martin remembers me from the YARDBIRD, and says, "Good to see you again, Stern. How about helping me get my gear out of the jeep?"

"Sure," I answer and grab for the bedroll as Martin takes out his typewriter and camera bag. With a little fast talking I manage to get Sergeant Martin a bunking place inside of the school building. I merely convince the Sergeant Major that here was his opportunity to get his puss in the paper. So it doesn't take long for STARS AND STRIPES to occupy a snug little corner outside of Colonel Darby's room. The reporter becomes the most popular guy in camp. All the guys want to edge up to him to tell their stories. I guess it's natural for the men to be talkative with the press. Sergeant Martin is mostly impressed with J.B.'s story of being a Texan oil driller and his $1,000 a month haul from stud poker and dice. Sergeant Martin makes notes of this. "You might add," says J.B., "That I send the money to my wife in Pampa, Texas. She'll love to see it in the paper."

Pretty soon I find myself telling STARS AND STRIPES some stories of my own and secretly hoping Sergeant Martin might get my name in too.

CHAPTER 10

SENED STATION RAID

On February 11, 1943, the Rangers conducted their first solo night raid on a rail town in southern Tunisia. The main objectives of the Sened Station Raid, also referred to as the AEF Raid from the first letters of the fighting companies, were to gather intelligence and to shake up the encamped Italian forces, convincing them a much larger force was operating in the area. By staging a series of raids, it was hoped that German troops would be diverted away from the Allies' planned advance.

After 200 Rangers were trucked 24 miles away to a French outpost, they conducted a night march of 12 miles. The next day was spent observing Italian movements, then concealing themselves among boulders and brush until it was time to attack. Faces were blackened, belt buckles and dog tags silenced with adhesive tape, wool caps replaced steel helmets and bayonets were fixed. Every man was ordered to use his knife and bayonet as much as possible. The raiding force consisted of three line companies and a detachment of 81mm mortars. They moved out three companies abreast, toward positions within 500 yards of the outpost.

It was a cold and starry night as the Rangers advanced in a skirmish line, infiltrating within 200 yards of enemy positions until they were compromised. Sweeping through the camp while mortar teams blasted the rear of the Italian elements, the Rangers killed at least 100 and captured 11 more from the elite 10th Bersaglieri Regiment and crack Italian Centuro Division, who nicknamed the Rangers "Black Death" or *Morte Nera.* It was a turning point for the

A few days after the Rangers' successful night attack at Sened Station, the battalion is ordered into a nearby clearing and told to stand at attention. Major General Fredendall gives a short snappy speech, then pins 12 Silver Stars on Rangers "For performance above and beyond the line of duty." A surprised Colonel Darby is also awarded a Silver Star for his brave leadership.

PHIL STERN / U.S. ARMY SIGNAL CORPS

Rangers, as most of the fighting was brutal, close, man-to-man combat. As one Ranger recalled: "There was some pretty intense in-fighting there, but a man doesn't talk about what he does with a bayonet."

Phil wasn't in on the action this time, as he wouldn't have been able to use a camera at night. He took guff from some of the men who told of the Italians' screams for mercy: "*Non ferire!*" "*Non uccidere!*" (Don't hurt! Don't kill!). James Altieri writes of plunging his knife into one Italian's stomach over and over despite his cries for his mother, "*Mamma mia!*" He burned his bloodied undershirt when he returned to the Gafsa bivouac.

After 20 minutes of fighting the objective was secured. Suffering just one killed, Private First Class Elmer Garrison, who had his head blown off by a cannon, and 20 wounded, the Sened Station Raid was considered a textbook demonstration of the Rangers' capabilities. Over the radio the next day, Axis Sally* called the Rangers a bunch of gangsters and convicts, warning, "Every Ranger captured will be killed by his own knife." For this reason they never carried anything that would identify them as Rangers.

✳✳✳

FEBRUARY 11, 1943: STATION DE SENED, TUNISIA

One evening in Gafsa, J.B. and I are comfortably squatted in our pup tent discussing the finer points of stud poker. Considering that there's a war on this is a very pleasant activity. It's a form of relaxation that's necessary, if we're to do any decent work the next day. After a while we get groggy from talking and we both doze off. But not for long. Some guy pokes his head into our tent and hollers at J.B., "Hey, Straight Flush! Get on the ball. A, E and F Companies are alerted for a job, you're wanted for Communications. Old man's orders." J.B. growls at the guy and almost throws a C-ration can at him. Since we sleep with clothes on, it takes J.B. just a few moments to get on his shoes and coat and wobble out of the tent. I figure it's all a dry run. So I turn over and discover how wonderful a pup tent can be when the other guy isn't in it.

---

* 'Axis Sally' was a nickname given to the female radio announcers who broadcasted Axis propaganda in English during World War II.

Rangers make their way across uneven rugged hillside and rocky mountain during a maneuver in Arzew in late January 1943. The Rangers often surprised the enemy, who considered attacks from difficult directions improbable. Darby's men proved that the hard route achieves the best results.
PHIL STERN

Yep, in the morning I learn that A, E and F companies are on a raid somewhere near Sened. I missed out on this so all I can do now is to wait until the three companies return and get the dope from them. Colonel Darby and all the exec officers are out on the new detail. The remaining men loll around the schoolhouse gabbing and speculating about this new adventure. It's really very vague so far and we must find out more when the boys return. I'll bet Colonel Darby picked those companies for the job because the operation could be labeled simply, "The AEF," for the abbreviations of the companies.

All this day we wait. It gets on our nerves. No news yet. At night we figure the boys will probably get back by morning. Nothing happens during our wait except for a dogfight between the patrolling planes. Toward evening Nazi and G.I. planes streak

across the sky, zooming and twisting. We can hear occasional
bursts of machine gun fire and the two machines disappear over
the mountains. That's all. I don't know about the other guys but
I can't sleep during the night. My pup tent is comfortable and
luxurious with J.B. gone off. But I miss the guy and hope he
doesn't get hurt. Besides he owes me twenty bucks. Early in the
morning all the guys are up and waiting for something to happen.
It does. Colonel Darby's jeep comes down the road. The Colonel's
driving. He pulls into the courtyard. He's smiling and quite
happy. The old man needs a shave though. The gang gathers around
Darby to listen.

"Men, we've done it. The Italian outpost at Sened Station.
We've ripped the place to pieces and caught the garrison with
their pants down." The tension is now eased and Darby continues.
"All the boys are under the bridge down on Messerschmitt Lane.
The wounded are there too. We've lost only one man out of F
Company. I want all transportation men and vehicles out to that
bridge immediately. It's open country so be on the lookout for
planes and don't spare the throttle."

I hop on to one of the jeeps as it moves out of the courtyard.
Three trucks and an ambulance are on the way. We're out to pick
up the AEF and bring them home. The road here is made of dirt,
which is now dry and dusty like powder. Each vehicle leaves
behind a streak of dust that begins to look like a smoke screen.
My jeep hits about sixty miles an hour. Even the trucks are hell
bent to reach the bridge. Messerschmitt Lane is certainly marked
up by war scars. There are bomb craters, smashed trucks and
tanks. Our boys are waiting for us just about four miles down
this road. We must work fast.

My jeep is the first vehicle to reach the bridge. A few guys
are sitting on the span. The rest are down below. They are a
dirty, grimy looking gang of men. Most of the guys are sprawled
out on the ground sleeping and resting. Rifles, field packs and
other gear are strewn all over. A few men merely sit and stare
as though they don't believe the world is still in one piece.
Medics are dressing the wounded. The hurt guys smile and puff
their cigarettes as though nothing happened. There's Garland
Ladd of F Company. We call him "Gar," the Kentucky kid. Gar
gets his right leg shot off by an anti-tank shell. He could
just as well have been left up to those hills but our boys

1st Ranger Battalion Rangers stand atop a mountain overlooking a Tunisian village. This was shortly before the night raid against the Italian outpost at Sened Station in southern Tunisia.
PHIL STERN

tucked Gar into a shelter half and carried him back through nine miles of tough hiking and over the worst possible terrain. As the medics place him into the ambulance, Gar smiles at me and says, "Too bad you missed out on this job, Phil. We had a lot of fun."

J.B. shows up as the last truck is loaded. "Hello baby," says J.B. "I bet you thought I was going to skip out on that twenty I owe you. Well, I almost did. One of those 40mm shells clipped my woolen cap." Which can be clearly understood when I get a look at J.B.'s headpiece. "Just a little bit lower," J.B. adds, "My dandruff condition would be ended forever." You can't doubt

J.B.'s wisdom on this point. Seeing J.B. and the guys is great. I even forget to mention that the boys brought back twenty-three Italian prisoners from Sened Station. A special truck is coming for them. They're a funny looking lot. They all seem to be wearing a different type of uniform. Their clothes are somewhat worn and patched. They are healthy looking and bronzed from the desert sun. Military interrogators from the rear may get some interesting info from these guys.

It's like a celebration back at the Gafsa schoolhouse. The cooks prepare hot cakes and coffee for the AEF boys. And they can sure pack in the chow. In between gulps they must try and answer the questions about the raid. Sergeant Ralph Martin, the STARS AND STRIPES reporter, is still hanging around, makes notes of all the conversation. He considers the Sened Station Raid a break because there are no other newspapermen around. So Sergeant Martin is making the most of his scoop. At first there are questions and answers. After that each guy relates what happened to him. J.B. tells of how his section was bracketed by a field piece. "The shells kept landing closer and closer to us and when it seemed our number was up there was a concussion and a flash. One of the guys knocked out the gun with a hand grenade."

Denny Bergstrom explains that AEF reached their objective after driving twenty-four miles on the Gafsa-Macknassy road to an isolated French outpost. From there they marched fourteen miles all night over rugged and treacherous terrain, then waited undercover during the day until full darkness fell the next night. Readying for battle with blackened faces, dog tags taped down (to eliminate any noise that might alert their approach to the enemy), woolen skullcaps and fixed bayonets. "During the waiting period we were pretty tense," Denny says "But the tension was relieved when three Arabs showed up right on our front line and tried to sell us oranges and eggs. Naturally we weren't taking any chances so we put the three Arabs under guard until after the attack."

Corporal Bob Halliday used to be a crooner in Syracuse. He's also one of the AEF men. "The attack came off as complete surprise," Halliday says, "The Italians could be seen running around in their underwear. Their officers grabbed motor bikes and crammed to the rear." Private First Class Imre Birgo, the Dead End kid, complains that an Italian concussion grenade landed

Shell Fire Mountain: The battle for the high ground at El Guettar from the vantage point astride
Djebel el Ank Pass. Rangers watch American artillery landing upon withdrawing enemy forces.
The Rangers had just captured the rocky mountain pass after a surprise dawn attack.
PHIL STERN

right by him and picked him up and laid him down three feet away.
"I got so damn mad, I grabbed a Tommy gun, waded in and tried to
find the guy who threw that pineapple." Biro adds, "Maybe I
didn't get the guy but I knocked off a couple of his cousins."
    At one point in the action Darby called Captain Max Schneider
on the radio asking how many prisoners he had taken. He said two
then the radio went out. Darby asked him again. "I had two sir,"
said Schneider. In the short time those two Eyeties tried to get
away so the Captain fired two shots and that was that.

Dick Bevin, a kid from Iowa, is part of one of our mortar crews. On the AEF deal, he crawled up to the most forward position to radio back for directions. Dick points out, "I get my eyes glued on a pillbox. I radio back the position and tell my crew, 'Throw in the kitchen sink.' And believe me they do. One pillbox totally disappears."

They figure the enemy death count at fifty with many more wounded, and eleven soldiers of the famed 10th Bersaglieri Regiment were captured. From them on the Eyties called the First Battalion Rangers "Morte Nera" or Black Death.

The AEF raid on Sened Station makes quite an impression on the big boys in the rear echelons. Darby said it was looked on as one of the most brilliant night attacks in the war so far. One day after the operation, the whole battalion is ordered out into a nearby wood. We stand at attention. The battalion's formation is such that we're surrounding a square area. General Fredendall, his staff and Colonel Darby walk into the square. Colonel Darby introduces the General to us where upon Fredendall gives us a short snappy speech on the great jobs done to the Italian outpost at Sened. The General then announces that he will award twelve Silver Stars to those men who were recommended "For performance above and beyond line of duty." The big surprise is at the end when the two-star General says, "This is not on the agenda and Colonel Darby knows nothing of it. I'm sure you boys will agree that Colonel Darby is deserving of a Silver Star for his active participation and brave leadership of the Sened Station Raid." Colonel Darby looks very proud as General Fredendall pins on the medal.

I should note - General Fredendall is in command of the Second Army Corps. He dresses informally at the front. He wears the tackiest outfit which consists of a combat jacket, a pair of long baggy pants and a woolen skull cap of course. Adding to this front line medal presentation, we hear the rumbling of an artillery duel in the distance.

The General's command car pulls out of the wood in a cloud of dust. The guys who get medals are congratulated and kidded by the rest of the men. We're a lucky Battalion so far.

Like many outfits, the Rangers had our own Poet Laureate and a darned good rifleman too. Private First Class Robert Dunn was known to quote from the Bible and Kipling and recite homemade verses to his tent mate. The tall, sinewy blond hailed from the Arkansas foothills of the Osarks and had a marvelous command of the English language which he used profusely. He wrote a poem after the successful Sened Station Raid.

Ballad of an Old Ranger

"On the Raid" (an extract)

Come Lad, Bring my Pipe and sit here on my knee
Ah, but I'm old, Come light it up for me.
My tale is what happened back in '43
T'was a gory battle as you soon shall see.

T'was a long cold ride that night to our rendezvous
24 to ride, 14 to hike before dawn broke through.
Aye lad, a long old hike and a tiresome one.
But we reached our point with the rising sun.

Sleep, little trooper? In no man's land?
We all stayed awake with guns in hand.
We lay there all day and all were chilled,
Canteens empty, stomachs unfilled.

At four p.m. the order came through,
To get ready to march to a position new.
Dog tired we marched over hill and dale
And stopped in a ditch in a busy vale.

With tense eager eyes we watched the moon sink low
And when it came, "On your feet. Let's go!"
We silently filed through a rocky pass
Into a valley matted with dewy grass.

Our objective, a wop held hill a mile away
Foreboding, grim, distant and gray.
None knew what the enemy held in store
Were they alerted or not? What was the score?

A machine gun nest (by bad luck in our path)
Was first to receive a shrapnel bath.
Close work now with bayonet and knife,
Rifle butt too, took its toll of life.

Screams of wounded foe were heard near and far
mid the staccato burst from the B.A.R.
Our mortar shells screamed overhead
Harmonizing with the final rattling breath drawn by the
dead

Our wounded lads were quite a few
Some bad, some slight they all came through,
Ah that long march back with them in tow
Fourteen miles we had to go.

Night fell, our trucks came in at last
Drive we said, they drove them fast
Ah, the olive grove, our pup tents there
The smell of coffee filled the air.

Ah, little trooper dream on, of gilded knight
I pray you never spend such a gruesome night
As when we went out on that little spree,
way back there in '43.

Written on an outpost March 6, 1943
by Pfc Robert C. Dunn, Company F

CHAPTER 11

TUNISIAN CAMPAIGN

The Tunisian Campaign was a series of battles fought between Axis and Allied forces in Tunisia during the winter and spring of 1943. These battles constituted the first significant engagements between the American and German forces during World War II.

In his book *An Army at Dawn: the War in North Africa, 1942–1943*, author Rick Atkinson wrote: "North Africa was a pivot point in American history, the place where the United States began to act like a great power – militarily, diplomatically, strategically, and tactically."

For those back home, North Africa and the Mediterranean seemed to be the least remembered campaign, even though it proved to be one of the key turning points in the Allied war against the Axis forces. Many factors came into play. One was a front line that extended from Gafsa southeast past El Guettar in towns with difficult, unromantic names such as Djebel el Ank, Bou Chebka and Sidi Bou Zid, along with confusing retreats and movements. Chronic supply shortages and transport problems led to several indecisive victories.

A sentry on patrol watches an enemy tank column burn near El Guettar in the distance. This was caused by rapid American artillery fire – so accurate the Axis troops thought the guns were automatically fed.

PHIL STERN

Phil didn't care much for the staged group shots of guys posing standing around. He preferred action or candid unguarded moments. Yet this shot taken in Tunisia seems to capture the various personalities that make up the Rangers, from goofy to composed and pensive. December 1942.
PHIL STERN

Operation *Torch* had taken the Germans by surprise, causing them to initiate a massive build-up in North Africa. The 10th Panzer Division, fresh from defeat by the Russians, were folded into the 5th Panzer Division in Tunisia under Generaloberst Hans-Jürgen von Arnim. Eisenhower's plans were to seize Tunisia before other German armies could link up. Discord between German General Erwin Rommel and von Arnim helped the Allied effort.

Two days after the Sened Station Raid, Axis forces consisting of German and Italian units led by von Arnim attacked the U.S. II Corps at Sidi Bou Zid. Under intense fire, orders were given to evacuate Gafsa. Forced into rearguard action, the 1st Ranger Battalion was left in chaos with little ammunition and weapons to fight off German Tiger tanks. Finding higher ground, a few days later Phil and a few Rangers captured a dozen German field police.

During the subsequent Battle of Kasserine Pass (February 19–24, 1943), a two-mile wide pass in the Atlas Mountains in west–central Tunisia leading to the American supply dump at Tébessa, Rommel's Panzers tore apart American units, including the 168th Regimental Combat Team.

After the American disaster at Kasserine Pass, General Eisenhower replaced the theater commander Major General Lloyd Fredendall with General George

Patton. Under his command they would capture Gafsa, El Guettar and hundreds of Italians of the Centauro Armored Division at Djebel el Ank.

With exemplary training and cohesion as a team, the Rangers were at their peak in North Africa. The taking of Djebel el Ank Pass on March 21, 1943, was the last use of the 1st Ranger Battalion in an authentic Ranger operation in North Africa. Ironically, the gains made in that action were given up within 48 hours when the Germans launched a counterattack culminating in the Battle of El Guettar (March 23 – April 3, 1943).

✳✳✳

FEBRUARY 14–MARCH 23, 1943

The brass thought the Rangers did such a swell job at Sened, a second raid was scheduled for the next day, February 14, in Djebel el Ank, a mountain pass about four miles east of El Guettar. Before we could get things moving we were ordered to retreat from Gafsa. Sent to rear guard instead of our usual front spearhead attacks we were then told to stay for four more hours after the others left. It soon got dark and very chilly. That's how the desert works. Freezing cold at night then hot as hell in the day. Can't make up its mind. We could hear the enemy approaching from the south so Darbo sent out some scouts. We heard what sounded like the advancing rumble of vehicles, then laughter. Turns out the enemy was a herd of two hundred camels kicking rocks as they moved along. They were more harmless than the other option. I'll take them any day over the Jerries. Our march resumed out of Gafsa toward Kasserine Pass.

We heard General Eisenhower had been in the vicinity. He was having "issues" with General Fredendall. That wasn't the biggest commotion though. Talk was Ike had a WAAC driver. Now that impressed us.

NEXT PAGES Despite all his cajoling and persuasiveness, Phil could not entice a group of captured P.O.W.s to cheerfully pose like movie versions of themselves. The prisoners, German secret police, or *Feldpolizei*, were Rommel's crack Afrika Korps, the first of the Jerries to fall into Ranger hands. Eventually some cigarettes persuaded the arrogant prisoners to play along.
PHIL STERN

Continuing our marching toward Kasserine into Fériana, we came across a brothel. One of the Rangers, an ex-bookie who also ran whorehouses in New York, was the first to discover the amenities.

On the American retreat in Tunis, soldiers began evacuating. They picked up forty French prostitutes from the brothel and loaded them on a truck moving toward the next strong point at Dernaia Pass.

The Germans and Italians were hunkered down at the gates of Fériana so we moved to high ground along the Fériana-Tébessa Road. Our orders were to defend Dernaia Pass to stop the capture of the Allied base, the well-stocked supply dump in Tébessa. Our new line was near Thelepte Airfield. There were long periods of enemy shelling. We only had a few tanks, some vehicles, small arms and sticky bombs.

We made it up to a little point near Gafsa where we were still holding our position. A couple of us were out on patrol when up came a brace of German jeeps filled with German Feldpolizei (Nazi military police). Two enemy personnel cars, a Volkswagen and a truck approached our position. I guess they thought they had run us out of the country already because inside their jeeps were direction signs to Algiers and Constantine.

Eight German prisoners were taken. They were all non-coms except one officer. He was out of the movies and out of the world. You know, one of those arrogant characters. I took his Luger away from him and was going to blow his guts out but I just couldn't do it. He was too close. So instead I thanked him for the gun and ordered him to surrender in my best Brooklyn Yiddish. I think he would have preferred being killed better. I never saw a guy deflate so fast. He turned yellow. His humiliation was lovely.

ABOVE RIGHT Fritzi had been a mascot for a unit in Rommel's Afrika Korps but was adopted by the Rangers. Phil worked up his Hollywood magic, crafting a background of barbed wire and a prisoner of war sign for the little pup.
PHIL STERN

RIGHT Captain Chuck Shunstrom inspects the marksmanship of E Company. The gun was a 37mm antitank used during action at Dernaia Pass. The occupants of the jeep were German military police dressed for duty at Tébessa, which they thought was still in Rommel's hands.

The loudest German prisoner was of the canine variety, a terrified little mutt, a dachshund, that wouldn't stop barking. She was the mascot for the Afrika Korps' 10th Panzer Division. Rommel had named her "Fritzi." I fixed up a barbed-wire prison camp à la Hollywood style and posed her standing up behind it pretending to hold on. Although we called her a Nazi Bitch she was not a storm Führer. She was a cute puppy dog. We fed her C-rations and put her in a tool kit to sleep. After three days of food, sleep and humane treatment we indoctrinated her to the Allied cause. She became attached to our kitchen truck. I guess she's still with the kitchen.

Later we were sent out on patrol into German lines toward Dernaia. We thought we heard what sounded like five hundred Nazis marching on us during the night. Turned out to be rows of G.I. oil cans knocking around the airport. We stretched out on miles of flat desert. We had good observation of the German positions. We were told to defend the Dernaia Pass until the Battle of Kasserine was over.

REST PERIOD

Around the first of March we were relieved by the 60th Infantry. It was a welcome rest period for the battalion. We moved to an area near El Kouif, set up camp and dined on powdered eggs and Spam.

I took off to Algiers to deliver film. In order to develop the negatives in the field I bring chemicals in little containers and shake 'em. Next, I deliver them to the coast about once a week to transfer radiophoto images. While I'm shooting, I write the details in a little notebook for the captions. The who, what, when and where. I usually bring forty rolls of film. That's a lot of cash so I only take a picture when I think it's important or see a story start to happen. I think I have a good eye to spot that picture that'll tell a tale for the folks back home. I'm not a big fan of a bunch of guys standing with their arms around each other. It's a bunch of shit. All the same stuff. It's boring. The secret is knowing where to look and where to frame the shot. Maybe catch somebody's movement to get some backstory, like a three-act play. I like to think I do art, not photography.

"Radio th' ol' man we'll be late on account of a thousand-mile detour."

ABOVE LEFT A trip to Algiers in khakis. Long before the advent of instant photographs, the process of taking pictures and developing them under less than ideal wartime conditions was not only tricky, it was downright dangerous. It often took Phil several hours to get from the battlefield to a civilized town and back for the purposes of developing and purchasing film.
U.S. ARMY

ABOVE RIGHT When Patton replaced Fredendall in North Africa on March 6, Phil and several others were fined $25 and a night in the slammer after Patton caught them without helmets. Editorial cartoonist Bill Mauldin created this spoof on the fines with the famous comic characters, Willie and Joe, a couple of two unkempt dogfaces. Phil's handwritten postwar notes show that he still had not forgiven Patton.
BILL MAULDIN / PHIL STERN

By the time I return to El Kouif, the Battalion has already gone to the front. I finally locate the outfit just as they are moving on to the big push into Gafsa again.

As we're riding through the desert we hear Gafsa getting bombed and shelled by the Jerries. Around this time we learn General Eisenhower had replaced Lieutenant General Fredendall with General Patton. Old Blood and Guts caught me without a helmet

(along with several other Rangers). That was nothing compared to his verbal beating of a dozen Rangers wearing soft caps and no ties. For my infraction he fined me $25 and a night in the military slammer.

MARCH TO EL GUETTAR

We're trucked to Dernaia, where we're attached to the 1st Infantry Division. We take Gafsa, then are ordered to spearhead the attack on El Guettar. The roads were filled with wreckage. At one point during the night we march through rain and mountain passes to flank El Guettar and capture it. When we get there it looked like the enemy had already evacuated. As we set up camp, the German artillery opens up and starts shelling our position on a rocky plateau that overlooked their positions. Nearby there's a camel we named "Mushmouth," who loved to watch the shells burst.

We make our way around a funnel-shaped mountain pass named Djebel-el-Ank. We're bombed and strafed by German Stukas on both sides of the pass. Darby sends two Ranger squads to silence the 88mm gun. With his '03 Springfield rifle our ace sniper, Corporal Robert Bevan from Iowa, quickly knocks out a machine gun nest.

There was a lot of commotion and confusion. Darby called out on the radio for Lieutenant Shunstrom. He and his men of C Company climbed the ridge with grenades and bayonets. White flags began waving. Soon prisoners were being rounded up.

LEFT During the German attack though Kasserine Pass the Rangers were tasked with rear guarding troops evacuating from Fériana. Ahead of them was 24 miles of flat ground which had to be crossed to reach the next strongpoint at Dernaia Pass. Behind and on their flanks were enemy armored columns. With no tanks, and only a few bazookas and sticky grenades to fight with, Darby gave his inspired battle cry: "Onward we stagger and if the tanks come, may God help the tanks!"
PHIL STERN

NEXT PAGES A motley group of around 200 Italian prisoners marches towards El Guettar in the Tunisian hills. When the Rangers attacked, shouting shrill Indian calls, many at their position on the mountain pass of Djebel el Ank were caught off guard. Father Basil intervened, convincing the resisters to surrender in his best Italian.
PHIL STERN

PREVIOUS PAGES Phil explaining camera angles to Italian P.O.W.s in Gafsa, Tunisia. The happy looks on their faces might mean they had conceded to American ideas about Fascists and Nazis.

U.S. ARMY

ABOVE LEFT Major Ralph Ingersoll, publisher of *PM Magazine*, meets his former staff photographer Sergeant Phil Stern for the first time on the hilly terrain of El Guettar. He played an integral role in the Ghost Army, a tactical deception unit set up to fool the Nazis on the location of D-Day landings.

PHIL STERN

LEFT A raggedy crew of Italian P.O.W.s listen intently to Major Ingersoll. Captured at El Guettar, many had already lost faith in *Il Duce*, their leader, and were happy to be done fighting.

PHIL STERN

ABOVE Tunisian P.O.W. camp, March 1943. Utilizing his Italian, British chaplain Father Albert Basil persuaded an Italian officer to surrender his remaining men to avoid further bloodshed. They capitulated and even subsequently assisted in lifting mines in front of their positions.

PHIL STERN

ABOVE Rangers inspect the inside of the "enemy" tank which was finally back in the hands of the Allies. The British nicknamed these American light tanks "General Stuarts" after the American Civil War general. In the latter stages of the war, M3 light tanks were replaced with heavier Sherman tanks and operated largely as reconnaissance vehicles.

PHIL STERN

ABOVE RIGHT A Ranger dives head first into the M3 Stuart light tank that had been confiscated by the Germans, probably during the disastrous battle at Kasserine Pass or the Battle of Sidi Bou Zid, in February 1943, then pressed into service.

PHIL STERN

RIGHT Phil and a group of Rangers gather round to congratulate First Sergeant Donald "Butt" Torbett on the destruction of the "enemy" tank by F Company in Tunisia.

U.S. ARMY

The Ranger assault caught the Italians off guard. They were a sad lot, dressed in long overcoats to their ankles. Speaking in fluent Italian, British chaplin Father Basil, who had accompanied us on the raid, was able to convince the few resisters to surrender and their lives would be saved.

We began walking our prisoners, about two hundred, back to El Guettar through a twisty, mountainous little goat path. I had my cameras stashed under my field jacket ready to snap in an instant. To calm my nerves on what was a long and tense hike, I began singing the popular Italian folk song "Funiculì, Funiculà." The Italian prisoners took my cue and joined in.

As the morning sun began to rise on the rocky trail, an unexpected but interesting surprise awaited me. I bumped into my PM MAGAZINE editor Ralph Ingersoll for the first time. He'd hired me as a staff photographer in New York before the war. We'd never met back in the States so I introduced myself. At forty-one, he was an officer with the engineers who went up on the attack with the Rangers. We had a reunion of sorts on the battlefield. Our meeting didn't last long because the enemy began a counterattack. They threw in the works. Dive bombers dropped stuff all over the place. Ralph was right in the middle of it. I saw a group of his boys blown to shreds all over a small hilly area.

We were lucky. No Rangers were killed in this battle.

✳✳✳

Ralph Ingersoll would later write a book about the Battle of El Guettar, *The Battle is the Payoff*. He also played a pivotal role in organizing a top-secret Army unit officially called the 23rd Headquarters Special Troops. Years after the war, it was referred to as the "Ghost Army." The top-secret, tactical deception unit, made up of former artists and soldiers, "deceived the enemy by utilizing inflatable tanks, sound effects, and other audacious fakery." They fooled the Nazis by distracting them with a build-up of fake armaments seemingly destined for Calais to cover up the real location of the D-Day invasion.

For days an Italian gun wreaked havoc on the 1st Battalion positions at Dernaia Pass. Hidden behind a small spur just east of Telepte Airfield, this gun was located by sharp-eyed Ranger observers, who directed Allied artillery fire on it. During their hasty retreat, the Italians further demolished the gun by blowing up the muzzle.
PHIL STERN

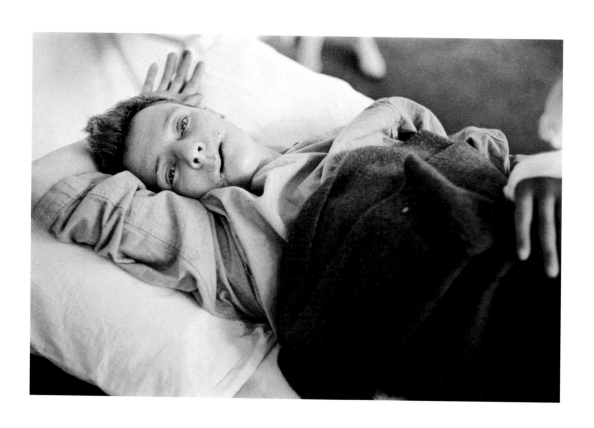

CHAPTER 12

WHAM! I'M HIT!

MARCH 23, 1943. EL GUETTAR VALLEY

The Germans didn't like losing so around March 23 a counterattack was initiated. I volunteered to join a party setting up an observation point. From my vantage point I could see down into the valley where Germans were forming to attack. I hitched a ride down.

The Germans' 10th and 21st Panzer divisions thrust up the valley toward us. Their tanks were made so they could sit and turn around and look both ways. They had 88mm artillery guns, which were very maneuverable. They were the scourge of the war and the scourge of the Americans. The Rangers' job was to direct artillery fire on to the tanks.

I was not in one of the American tanks. I was part of the troops scattered all over the place in no-man's-land, marching alongside

Tank boy: Phil managed to coax a little smile from a young tank man badly wounded in action. Overworked doctors at the 12th General Hospital allowed Phil to be in the room to take photos during surgery. The young lad's mouth had been torn to shreds by mortar shells. Plastic surgeons did their best to fix his smile.

PHIL STERN

the tanks with everyone else. The Germans began firing shells into what they thought would likely be good targets. A Ranger yelled out. We all ran to both sides of a rocky hillside. The radio operator calling in for artillery was overrun. Both he and Captain Martin were shot up while directing fire so Captain Saam and I took their places. We ran over to the radio operations position and starting directing fire. I was shot at a few times. Someone miscalculated the pattern of falling shells.

Maybe it wasn't so smart but I wanted to get some good action shots. I had just exposed a frame when an 88mm round shell came in real fast, blowing up right where I was. The explosion knocked me out, shattered my leg and left a big flesh wound. Shrapnel lacerated my neck and tore up my right hand but I was able to rip open a sulfanilamide pack with my teeth and left hand and pour antibiotic on my wounds.

I was gotten, so to speak. The First Ranger Battalion medics stopped the blood flow and got me to a nearby field hospital. Because my officer was shot, there was space for me on that jeep. That's the way it goes, I guess. They loaded me on an ambulance to take me to a field hospital. It was a rough ride, bouncing around from the bombing and shelling. I could see holes in the sides of the jeep. When we arrived at the aid station, I remember being given the last rites from the Army chaplain. Fine thing! I told him I had to decline because I still had five more payments to make on my car. Another ride took me to an evacuation hospital in Tunisia, where I was given initial surgery then driven to the airport and flown to the 12th General Hospital in Morocco.

My right hand was half ripped off, my neck and right arm were disabled, and my left leg was shattered. My hand was half on, half off. The tendons that work your fingers and the nerve which

RIGHT TOP When Phil saw this his photo in *Stars and Stripes* with a caption describing his demise, he was unsure if he was dead, delirious or back in Brooklyn. *"This is the last photograph by Sgt. Phil Stern that will appear in the* Stars and Stripes ... *Sgt. Stern took some of the best soldier photographs we have ever seen. We miss him on our staff."*
PHIL STERN

FAR RIGHT March 23, 1943, in El Guettar Valley. Phil volunteered to accompany American tanks marching towards the approaching Panzer divisions. Very soon after taking this photo, Stern was hit by 88mm shell fire from the German Panzers.
PHIL STERN

rs On The March

operates the arm were lacerated. The surgeons stitched each tendon together again. I was young and healed fast which was good because it was my camera hand. They had it working better than before!

At that time the big military hospitals were staffed by a hospital from an American city. This particular hospital was staffed by Massachusetts General. It was normal in some cases to staff an entire military hospital by one in the U.S. My surgeon, Lieutenant Colonel Harvey S. Allen, M.C., was a hand expert. He was a miracle worker.

While I was recuperating in hospital someone, a nurse I believe, showed me a copy of STARS AND STRIPES with a photograph I had taken in North Africa. I didn't even remember taking it. It was right before I was hit by the Panzers. The caption read:

> This is the last photo taken by Sgt. Phil Stern that will appear in the Stars and Stripes. ... Sgt. Stern took some of the best soldier photographs we have ever seen. We miss him on our staff. - Editor

I had an eerie feeling and got a little scared. The way the caption read it sounded as if I had been killed. Then it flattered me and went on to say what great photos I had taken and how much I'd be missed, so it wasn't all bad. I bet they'll feel pretty dopey when they see me walking around in a couple of weeks.

HOSPITAL LIFE

For three weeks I was in God-awful pain. There was a colorful cast of characters roaming around the hospital. I met Captain Reidy who liked to draw cartoons on everyone's casts. A wounded kid by the name of Solomon had the bad fortune of having his arm

Army doctors were there to aid the Rangers but also the innocent ones caught in the crossfire. Lieutenant John J. Goldstein, Medical Corps, from Georgia, administers treatment in the form of a bandage to an injured Arab child who was run over by a truck when the Germans counterattacked at El Guettar.

in a cast pointing up in a perfect "Heil Hitler" salute. He was thoroughly embarrassed.

The amputations ward, or as some called it, the Stump Brigade, was a solemn place. I felt lucky that I still had all my appendages (for now).

As I began feeling better I was itching to take some photos. I found a camera and got the okay to observe and take a couple pictures of the docs in action. Sometimes they'd spend between four and six hours on each soldier. They're overworked like all of us but we're lucky to have them to fix us up. One poor guy, a seventeen-year old American tank man, was badly shot up by mortar shells. His face was torn to shreds and the plastic surgeons were trying to piece it back together. They let me in the room to take some shots of the surgeons working on his mouth. They did their best to fix his smile. The result was less than perfect - thick scars and a misshapen mouth. I was able to coax a small smile out of him. Don't know what happened to that kid.

Since I was told I could have all the ice cream I wanted, I would frequently raid the ice box. The ice cream was needed for healing, "calcium," the nurses explained. It was given to the soldiers for medical reasons not dessert. Probably for morale but that was just fine with me.

As things seemed to be calming down, the Jerries launched a last ditch air raid over Oran. Anti-aircraft fire lit up the night sky. The Axis finally capitulated and surrendered in May.

Me and a few other fellas were transferred to Casablanca Military Hospital. There's a U.S. hospital train that runs between Oran, Algeria, Casablanca and French Morocco. I heard there were around seven military hospitals in the Casablanca area. That's a lot of wounded men.

Lieutenant Morton Horowitz came in one day. He was a medic. Got shot up aiding wounded boys in the Infantry. Another day, a little Arab kid was run over by a truck. Our grade A Army medics administered medical treatment in the form of a bandage.

Phil's Purple Heart medal received for wounds inflicted during the Battle of El Guettar on March 23, 1943.
PHIL STERN

I paid a visit to Arthur Spackman (1st Battalion, D Company), who was bedridden. We were in the same ward for five days before we found each other as we both bunked on either end. Art was wounded in the chest and leg when the Germans knocked him out with their 88s in El Guettar, two days after me. He still believes the U.S. Long Toms are more deadly. He's from Montana and the guys would kid him about being a sheepherder every time a sheep was in the area, which was almost all the time especially in the mountains. Thing is he was from the city of Butte and never saw any animals.

A guy named Paul Green was visiting the hospital and stops to talk to us. Says he's from Brooklyn so we figure he's all right. He's an Army reporter for STARS AND STRIPES so it's in his blood to ask us a bunch of questions. We don't mind. Not much else to do in the hospital. We spin a yarn telling him all about the Rangers and the Oran attack. Private James Barefoot (his real name), a tough Jew from New York, comes over and jabbers on about how he was armed with a submachine gun, pistol and grenades strung on his chest. Took forty-seven French prisoners in his first gun raid then proceeded to march them down the street. "We didn't lose a single man," he said. After Oran we tell him we lived like kings for a few days, on the beach in resort-like cabins and swell food. We tell Paul how after capturing Germans in Tunisia, we found a lot of American equipment on them: jeeps, revolvers, machine guns and C-rations. The Italians like to eat spaghetti but also tell us C-rations are "trés bon." The Germans, however, are happy with cabbage.

Since I was feeling better and things were fairly peaceful, I snuck out to Casablanca and did some sightseeing. I took a tour of the Sultan's Palace. In January the Sultan had met with President Roosevelt during the Casablanca Confe rence. We heard the Sultan (Mohammad V of Morocco) arranged for a group of important Jews to sneak into the palace hidden in a covered wagon so he could meet them away from the meddling eyes of the French.

Back in the hospital, I get a surprise visit from Colonel Egbert "Bert" White of STARS AND STRIPES. He walks right in and offers me a job. I wanted to let Colonel Darby know so I sent him a note. He got back to me quick.

HEADQUARTERS 1st RANGER BATTALION
AFO 302, U.S. Army – 8 June 1943
Sergeant Philip Stern
Stars and Stripes
AP #512, U.S. Army

My Dear Stern,
Received your note. I too am sorry we missed connecting as I wanted to talk to you!
As far as I'm concerned, Stern you did an excellent job with this organization from the day you joined us until the day you were wounded at El Guettar. So it is a pleasure to write you a letter of commendation, which you will find enclosed.
Here's wishing you luck, and I hope you make it. Please know that we miss you.
Sincerely,
William O. Darby

Lt. Col., 1st Ranger Bn. Commanding.
LETTER OF COMMENDATION
SUBJECT: Commendation
TO: Whom it may concern.

1.   Sgt. Philip Stern, 12091020 served continuously and honorably with this organization from 22 September 1942 until he was wounded in action at El Guettar, Tunisia on 23 March 1943.
2.   Sgt. Stern served in the operation's section as a photographer of this headquarters. His skill and enthusiasm as a photographer greatly contributed to the training of this organization for combat. He proved himself to be mentally alert, loyal and hardworking.
3.   In my opinion he has the qualifications to make it as a photographic officer in the Signal Corps.

Signed
William O. Darby
Lt. Colonel, 1st Ranger Bn.
Commanding.

CHAPTER 13

STARS AND STRIPES

JUNE 1943, ALGIERS

Taking advantage of my newly acquired limited duty status, I waited until I was sufficiently healed to begin working as an official STARS AND STRIPES photographer. Red tape from the upper echelons was holding things up, so I used some connections to get me on the staff. The connection was General Eisenhower. Ike, who inhabited offices a few buildings away in Algiers, was a fan of STARS AND STRIPES, having knocked down General Patton's order to gag the G.I. Newspaper. Said Ike publicly:

I welcome the publication of STARS AND STRIPES. We are a long way from home. Only people who have experienced the isolation inherent in extended military operations can fully appreciate the value to the soldier of news from

The editorial staff of *Stars and Stripes* pose for a group shot in the basement of the Agricole Building in Algiers, North Africa, in June 1943. The staffer on the right holds up the very first issue of the Mediterranean edition.
PHIL STERN

home and friends and the need for widespread coverage of our own activities. The newspaper staff will render inestimable value to our armed forces in North Africa and to the cause for which we fight.

American Soldiers are not in an imperious army. They are kids that are fearful and homesick and have lots to bitch about. STARS AND STRIPES is logically the healthy and logistically perfect mechanism to let off the steam.

I've paraphrased his words, which were personally said to the STARS AND STRIPES editorial staff at a lunch in our Algiers office. Ike actually invited himself to our canteen! I might add that we had two fabulous French chefs who cooked up objects d'art with the local produce combined with the G.I. rations (yep, they made sumptuous omelets out of that frigging G.I. powdered eggs!). Our STARS AND STRIPES Café was known all over the North Africa Theater as having the best meals on the continent. It was so good that Ike periodically arranged lunches at STARS AND STRIPES for visiting dignitaries like senators and even First Lady Eleanor Roosevelt on one occasion.

Prior to meeting my new co-workers, I was hanging around Casablanca for a while. After being discharged from the hospital my cameras finally caught up with me from El Guettar. I thought they'd been tossed out or busted up. The Leica I had under my jacket now had a shrapnel hole in the back. That camera was positioned right in front on my heart. It saved my life!

I finally get orders to fly to Algiers to meet all my new friends on the staff. Bert White is the oldest of the bunch. He worked on STARS AND STRIPES in World War I and started YANK MAGAZINE after Pearl Harbor. Jack Fosie was at the SAN FRANCISCO

ABOVE RIGHT On Phil's sightseeing outing he visited the steep cobblestone stairs in Algiers also known as the Kasbah of Algiers. Rising 400 feet above the sea, the ancient steps were used as a backdrop in the 1938 film *Algiers* starring Hedy Lamarr and Charles Boyer.
PHIL STERN

RIGHT This little card signed by high command granted Phil access to any transportation to any unit in the Mediterranean theater of war. "I could go in an aircraft, tank, car, on a bicycle, didn't matter what. I could go any place I pleased that I thought would be interesting to the newspaper."
PHIL STERN

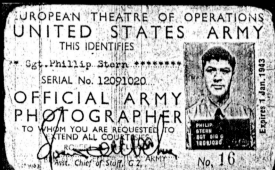

CHRONICLE before the war. Herbert Mitgang, Ralph Martin, the airsick reporter on the plane, Paul S. Green, Milton Lehman and Jack Belden are all ace reporters.

They were pretty shocked to learn I have never been to a bordello so I make my first visit to a whorehouse where I meet Madam Fox who introduces me to Paulette who is very affectionate but refuses to take payment. Later I walked up the famous Kasbah stairs in Algiers. For some reason they are known as Rue de Regarde.

LIMITED DUTY

I had what can be called a dream job. I was given a little card signed by high command granting me access to any transportation to any unit in the Mediterranean theater of war, space permitting. The powers that be were to cooperate with me in every way. I could go in an aircraft, tank, car, on a bicycle, didn't matter what. I could go any place I pleased that I thought would be interesting to the newspaper.

The War Department, the Signal Corps, to be specific, required combat photographers to use Speed Graphic 4x5 plate cameras. The film supplied was in the form of film packs or film holders, which were both unwieldy. The circumstances of war, the terrain, actions and general horror of a war drama made it so those were the most ludicrous cameras to use. I personally dumped two of those cameras off Tunisian mountains into the plains of the desert. I did that only after I had my own cameras, a German 35mm camera and a larger reflex type camera. Those were easy and light to carry and took multiple pictures from one role of film instead of single plates from the bigger camera. They made my life much more pleasant.

My first assignment for STARS AND STRIPES was to be the invasion of Sicily. Before shipping out, I hitched a ride to the port city

After the Germans capitulated in May, and prior to the Sicilian invasion, Lieutenant Colonel William Darby, Captain Roy Murray and Major General Terry Allen gathered in Zeralda, Algiers to celebrate the first anniversary of the Rangers' formation with a birthday cake. In one year the battalion had grown to three. June 19, 1943.
PHIL STERN

of Mostaganem, northwest of Algeria, to meet up
with Clinton Green in the Ordnance Group. Some
of the boys who saw the ten star show of the
Canastel band on Thursday night say it was the
best thing ever to come out of that place.
Captain Green gets me all my supplies, weapons
and ammunition. I take along a cot and bedroll.

About twenty-four troop ships are anchored in
Oran as I board the U.S.S. SUSAN B. ANTHONY. The
320th Barrage Balloon Battalion and the 45th
Infantry Division are assembling. The Seventh
Army guys and 3rd Battalion Rangers mill around.
I pack my gear into the General's jeep and ready
the countdown for the "Big Assignment."

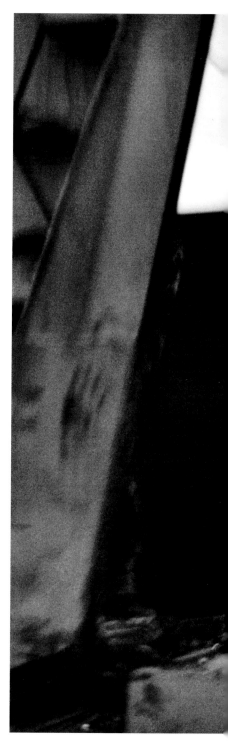

ABOVE Like all the Rangers and war correspondents, Phil wore his 1st
Ranger Battalion and *Stars and Stripes* patches with pride.
PHIL STERN

RIGHT Against a backdrop of billowing smoke, an American carrying his
rifle is caught by a quick flash of the camera as he hits the beach during a
practice landing exercise somewhere in North Africa. This training would
be critical a month later during the invasion of Sicily.
PHIL STERN

CHAPTER 14

OPERATION *HUSKY*

Plans to invade Sicily were already set in motion prior to the Axis surrender in Tunis, North Africa on May 13, 1943. The decision was confirmed at the Casablanca Conference in January 1943 between President Franklin D. Roosevelt and Prime Minister Winston Churchill. Codenamed *Husky*, the main goal of the operation was the removal of the Italian and German military and control of the Mediterranean shipping lanes. Sicily, an island the size of Vermont, would be the staging area for the larger drive into mainland Italy, the "soft underbelly of Europe."

The invasion of Sicily was the largest amphibious operation of World War II in terms of the size of the landing zone, with seven Allied divisions engaged in the assault waves. It was the first major Allied assault on German-occupied Europe. A total of 150,000 troops, 3,000 ships and 4,000 aircraft would strike the rugged southern and eastern coasts of Sicily, beginning in the early morning hours of July 10, 1943.

After leading the 1st Battalion Rangers through decisive battles against the formidable Axis forces during the Tunisian Campaign, Colonel Darby was

Rifles at the ready, Rangers offloading from a landing craft in later assault waves meet with little enemy resistance as they disembark near Licata Beach, Sicily, 1943.
PHIL STERN

ordered to create, recruit and train two additional Ranger battalions in just six weeks. Consisting of the 1st, 3rd and 4th Ranger battalions, the newly formed Darby Ranger Force would spearhead the invasion. American forces landed at Licata, Gela and Scoglitti beaches, with heavy resistance at Gela, a sleepy fishing community of 30,000 with gun positions located on a 150-foot-high hill.

✳✳✳

JULY 10, 1943 SICILY

It was still dark onboard the U.S.S. SUSAN B. ANTHONY as we approached the coast of Sicily near the town of Scoglitti. Almost immediately a voice through the loudspeaker made the announcement: "Gentlemen, proceed with disembarkation," or some big word like that. They could just as well have said, "Get the hell over the side!" We all climbed down the rope ladders into the boats. The soldiers carried only packs with three K-rations and their rifles. The sea was very rough. We expected to get hit at any minute. By 0400 enemy planes were attacking the ships. We sat there, huddled down to protect us from flying metal. But I had to get pictures. My head was bobbing up and down. I made an exposure and ducked. Everybody was very quiet except the naval officer in charge. He was joking all the time. Gags like "Well, boys you'll be having ravioli in a couple of hours." It started

PREVIOUS PAGES American barrage balloons were first tested in battle in Sicily, July 1943 where they were deployed to shield men and material from enemy aircraft. They would later appear over the beaches of northwestern France with the U.S. Army's 320th Barrage Balloon Battalion, the first segregated unit of black soldiers to man barrage balloons and the only African-American combat unit to take part in the D-Day invasion, coming in on the third wave at Omaha Beach in Normandy.
PHIL STERN

RIGHT The youngest participant in the invasion of Sicily was likely 15-year-old sailor Jimmy E. Conaway of Dillindale, Ohio. He joined the Navy giving his age as 17. His cover was safe until he hit the Atlantic Ocean. His skipper received a wire from the Navy ordering Jim's active duty stopped and that he be discharged on returning to the States, but it was too late – the troopship was invasion bound. He later stated he'd had enough of war: "I guess I'll go back home and get a job in the coal mine where dad works."
PHIL STERN

ABOVE The U.S.S. *Susan B. Anthony* set sail for Sicily on July 5, 1943, carrying the U.S. 3rd Ranger
Battalion and Patton's Seventh Army. Strong winds and a choppy sea made for a rough ride.
Approaching the coastal town of Scoglitti, she landed men and materiel while fighting off enemy
air attacks. A year later she would carry 2,500 reinforcements to Omaha Beach on D-Day.
PHIL STERN

RIGHT Darby addresses troops about the invasion of Sicily. The 1st and 4th Ranger Battalions,
along with 1st Division, would land on Gela beachhead. Because of the rough seas, after midnight
on July 10 men were seasick and vomiting. Nearing the shore gunboat guides flashed their lights
and shouted to the men on the first wave, "Go straight ahead and good luck!"
PHIL STERN

NEXT PAGES All smiles and nerves on board this Higgins boat. Lessons learned from the invasion
of Arzew eight months earlier would come in handy for the Rangers as they made their approach
to Licata Beach. July 10, 1943.
PHIL STERN

PREVIOUS PAGES First wave of Rangers assaulting the beachhead in Sicily, July 10, 1943. The landing took place on Falconara Beach near Punta Duc Rocche, a small beach between Licata and Gela. A British sailor can be seen in the foreground on the landing craft. Americans were short on ships, so the British supplied the Yanks with a full crew.

PHIL STERN

ABOVE "We got most of the equipment and vehicles to the beach without a problem. There was a little opposition from the Italians. Some guys were shot but luckily not too many. The fellows over in Gela had a tough time. Fate had a big hand in this," recalled Phil.

PHIL STERN

RIGHT The aftermath of the successful Allied landings on Sicily. A wounded soldier captured for posterity by Phil.

PHIL STERN

getting light about 0530. We pulled in closer to the beach to proceed with landing operations when the shore batteries opened up. We turned, maneuvered and the whole convoy got out of range while the naval guns roared. It was wonderful how accurate they were. The Navy gave us the go ahead signal and we began landing operations. As the troop transport edged on to the beach, bombs and shellfire were exploding all around and planes were strafing the deck. Naturally the boys were a little uneasy. It was very light then, about 0630. The waves were about ten feet high near the shore. The boat grounded and we all hopped out. The water came up to my waist. It felt swell after all the sweating we'd gone through. It made me feel relaxed, like a kid in wading pool. But I had to worry about my camera. I held it above my head like the others held their rifles.

I came in on the first wave along with Patton's Seventh Army while the 3rd Ranger Battalion led by Major Dammer landed in Licata. A lot of guys had already reached the shore. Our sector wasn't barraged as bad as the other points but there were casualties. Luckily all I got was a couple of sand tick bites. It was like a huge anthill and the dunes were practically squirting sand as our forces raised a hospital, kitchen and headquarters tents. A lot of vehicles, not the amphibious ones, but the regular land type, were off-loaded and grinding through the sand. There was wonderful visibility. Everybody kept looking up waiting for those German planes to appear but our ack-acks discouraged further airplane interruptions. Sand was flying all over the beach as the guys dug foxholes. The amazing thing was that the planes never did come over. Once we made it on to the beach and dry land we started over the dunes to see what the country was like then headed toward town.

ABOVE RIGHT A half-teed-up Italian offers bread and wine from a depleted bottle to the Rangers, who made him test it out first to be sure the Nazis hadn't poisoned it as they retreated.
PHIL STERN

RIGHT L.S.T.s from the mother ship motor towards the Sicilian coast. Overhead are spotter planes. "I exposed this frame about 5:30 the morning of the invasion. We weren't too far out. The Germans knew we were coming but they didn't know exactly where we planned to land," Phil later recalled.
PHIL STERN

TOP The corpse of a charred Italian pilot near his crashed plane, a Fiat CR.42 Falco. The Italian-made CR.42s were employed as a last-ditch effort against the Allied landings. July 1943.
PHIL STERN

ABOVE The US Liberty ship S.S. *Robert Rowan* explodes after being hit by German dive-bombers off the coast of Gela, Sicily, on July 11, 1943. Flames ignited the ammunition in the cargo holds. An explosion tore the ship in half, sending a column of smoke thousands of feet into the sky, with pieces of metal scattered across the sea.
U.S. ARMY SIGNAL CORPS

"Heading inland from the beach it was hot as hell. We broke up into squares and were walking towards Comiso when we came upon this German weapons carrier and the charred bodies of two German soldiers among the twisted wreckage. American gunfire had set off the explosives and ammo it was carrying," remembered Phil.

PHIL STERN

TOP Happy to be alive, Phil attempts to ride on a mule-drawn cart in Gela.
PHIL STERN / U.S. ARMY

ABOVE RIGHT Phil Stern with farmer Tom Adamo and his family in Comiso. Adamo tried to
convince Phil to desert the Army and marry his 17-year-old daughter, Angelina, and avoid getting
killed. He was tempted, but decided to stick with the Army.
U.S. ARMY

ABOVE LEFT There were a lot of dogs in Sicily, and the one place they could stay cool and keep
their paws from burning up was hiding or walking in the shade underneath the horse-drawn
wagons.
PHIL STERN

As we made our way inland the sand suddenly disappeared, dunes flattened into fertile plains and the ground became hard and firm. The first civilized things we saw were grape bushes and olive orchards. The roads were shiny white and they glistened in the sun. When the civilians and soldiers saw our trucks on the roads, they were amazed. "There are no roads from North Africa. How did you get here?" they asked, confused about how we were able to come ashore with all these men and machines.

Along a narrow road I saw a ragged Italian farmer. He didn't have a gun so I went up to him and said in my best Brooklyn Italian, "Buongiorno!" What did he say in return? "Hiya keed." It turned out his name was Tom (Gaetano) Adamo. He had lived in Hackensack, New Jersey, for twenty years, pressing women's dresses. His sisters still live there. With the money he accumulated through the years, he was able to return to Sicily and buy a house and a farm. "I lived the life of a millionaire until the damnable Nazis infested our land," said Tom. He was very happy that the Americans had come. "Damn right," he said. "Fascists no good. No movies here. In America every corner I see movies. I was treated okay in America." Tom was determined to treat Americans well. He gave me wine, some pears and peaches. I was introduced to the whole family and gave them some chewing gum and sugar. Except for the fruit, garlic and tomatoes the people had nothing but crude dark bread and wine.

After talking to Tom for a while he suggested I desert the Army to avoid getting killed because it's very likely to happen. Instead, I should marry his seventeen-year-old daughter Angelina. It was an interesting proposition and a tough choice to make: stay with the family and with Angelina or return with my cameras to America. I thought about it for a short while. You need to be brave to be a deserter and I am not brave so I decided to stick it out with the Army.

The American boys of Italian descent were really in their heyday. They could ask and answer questions in Italian and there were plenty of both. In one section there was an "American Street," where many of the soldiers' relatives lived. In the Sicilian town of Mezzojuso, an Army corporal named Salvatore di Marco found his home and family pretty much as he left them fifteen years ago when he sailed for America. One old man named Sam Cheli, who used to sharpen knives in New York City before returning to Sicily, had

this to say: "Of course we are happy to see you Americans but you should have come three years ago. Fascist propaganda said Americans were very vicious and kill people without mercy."

Well, whatever it is going on here certainly is different from what they expected. I'll never forget the medics' First Aid Station. The locals gave us wine and food. They'd drink it first to show it was safe, that the Germans hadn't poisoned it on their retreat.

On the road to Comiso, I hitched a ride on a half-track with the 1st Infantry. There were pictures of Mussolini all over the place. He was "Il Duce," their Führer, but the civilians seemed pretty happy to see us standing on the sidewalks, cheering and waving as we walked and drove by. They considered us Americans as liberators, not conquerors. As we rolled into town loudspeakers were blaring in Italian instructing all civilians to immediately report and turn in all firearms at the local post office. And they did, without much resistance.

Many of the people greeted us with Fascist salutes. I guess they didn't think there was any other manner of greeting a military force. Some people raised both hands to surrender. We waved to them in return. Boy, were they happy to see us.

We were in Comiso for about forty-five minutes before moving out again. I was accompanying an anti-tank unit assigned to capture the nearby airfield. About five minutes later the enemy opened fire. We were shot at by their artillery. We all piled out of the half-tracks and hit the gullies. We were shelled for half an hour then the infantry finally got the guns. We got back

---

PREVIOUS PAGES As they entered the town as liberators, American soldiers, shouting through loudspeakers, instructed residents and resisters to report immediately to the City Hall to turn in all their firearms. On Palazzo Occhipinti, Italians line up with hands raised high in front of a Fascist backdrop of *Vincere* stenciled on the wall – it means "win" or "conquer."
PHIL STERN

ABOVE LEFT American troops entering the Sicilian town of Comiso. Cheering civilians lined the sidewalks to greet American patrols, waving handkerchiefs and giving the Nazi salute. "That's what they were used to so they thought it was normal," later recalled Phil.
PHIL STERN

LEFT Rangers ride on a military vehicle in front of the Church of San Giuseppe in Comiso.
PHIL STERN

PREVIOUS PAGES Rangers on patrol through the ancient streets of Sicily.
PHIL STERN

ABOVE Italian-speaking American soldiers in Sicily were given a rapturous welcome.
NATIONAL ARCHIVES

ABOVE RIGHT This photograph of an American G.I. being greeted by his Italian family in Sicily
was later reproduced in *Stars and Stripes*.
NATIONAL ARCHIVES

RIGHT Throughout Sicily drawings of Mussolini were painted and etched all over buildings and
walls. By the time the Allied forces arrived, he was no longer the leader of the Italians.
PHIL STERN

ABOVE Sicilian kid "Nick" Nicola quickly picks up the finer points of baseball from Sergeant Robert Zelina of Cleveland, Ohio. Playing the position of catcher is Private First Class Leo Podchasky of Eynon, Pennsylvania. Looking on with curiosity are two railway conductors.
PHIL STERN

ABOVE RIGHT Civilians queue up outside the temporary American headquarters to turn in their contraband firearms. Like the guns of most American farmers, the ones they fought with were the double-barreled buckshot kind.
PHIL STERN

RIGHT As the Rangers make their way inland, a Sicilian youth by the name of Giovanni Guillini obligingly draws a bucket of water from a crude well, offering to quench the thirst of weary American soldiers.
PHIL STERN

into the vehicle and came within two hundred yards of the airport when a jeep dashed out and a captain told us that the airport was not ours yet and there was going to be a big attack in about twenty minutes. We pulled right back quick, bivouacked right by a gasoline dump. Then I jumped into an unfinished foxhole about two feet deep. One bomb dropped about 120 feet away. You know what that means - the ground shakes and the shrapnel sings and you choke in the dust. This was the worst bombing I have ever been in. I saw myself back in the hospital with nurses running around with giant thermometers.

The bombers missed the dump completely, thankfully. We took off and came to a group of buildings, which had been used by a German

ABOVE When the fighting became more intense in North Africa and the Mediterranean, Bob Hope felt the need to entertain the troops on the front lines instead of safely at home on the radio. The former vaudevillian and his troupe were the first entertainers in North Africa since Rommel and the Italians had pulled out in May 1943.
PHIL STERN

ABOVE LEFT Hope and his crew found their largest audience of the whole war in Palermo, with 19,000 boys. The performers narrowly escaped when 100 Nazi Junker Ju 88s with a fighter escort dive-bombed the docks, destroying their hotel a few blocks away.
PHIL STERN

cadre. I found a Nazi paper and read up on their defeat in Tunisia. All of a sudden there was the zip, zip, zip of sniper fire. The Germans had been practicing for weeks in the area. We pulled out and into the nearest gulley. They let loose but failed to stop us. Then in a very academic manner we started clearing them out with .50 caliber machine gun fire. Tracer fire set the place afire and incendiary rifle grenades finished them off. There were weird howls from the snipers as they died.

As we moved along, we were joined by more German machine gun fire. We entered some gullies and took shelter for half an hour or so. A hundred feet from where we were standing, a bomb fell and the earth trembled. There were also some snipers who fired but gradually we managed to neutralize them. We walked in a row with machine guns, always careful to avoid snipers and minefields. We were very tense. Suddenly a metallic glint appeared in a window. We opened fire and for a few seconds there was only the sound of our machine guns. We approached the building and discovered a woman holding a pot in one hand, that was the reflection, and in the other arm she was cradling a baby torn by our shots. Both lay dead and bleeding, killed by a reaction of our nerves on edge. I did not know the war until that moment. But once inside, I realized the only way to endure it was not to think.

In one of the houses, which had been a hastily abandoned officer quarters, I found a treasure trove of souvenirs for which most Yanks have a weakness. In this case, they left me with a burden of objects. I found a complete snapshot history of one Nazi's war adventures. Among them poses of conquered Europeans and pictures, which revealed this German had been in Russia. "Have a look at these kids," I said, showing the guys. Among tender messages of love from "Rosa" at home were pictures of two young boys, already in uniform and squatting behind a wooden machine gun tripod playing the usual Teutonic war games.

More pictures depicted marching youngsters goose-stepping like their dads after 1918. I'm not sure but I think this officer's career is ended. One of the Germans, and it was probably him, ran in the direction of our armor and was undoubtedly mowed down. I examined the items in the house, found a compass and other stuff but hung properly in the latrine behind the house, I unfolded an excellent picture of their Führer.

Making our way to Gela, I learned Ralph Martin was down with malaria.* Too bad for him.

From Comiso we followed ongoing movements and battles through Catania to the southern town of Ragusa. The Germans were up in Palermo so we headed in that direction. There was some fighting to take the airport but there wasn't much enemy resistance as the Germans were retreating to the mainland. While there, a minor wound aggravated my more serious injuries from Tunisia. I made my way back to Licata Airport and hopped a ride back to the base at Algiers for more medical treatment. My arm and wrist were banged up and weakened from the strain in Sicily.

***

Adolf Hitler canceled a major offensive at Kursk a week after the initial landings, to divert forces to Italy, resulting in a significant reduction of German strength on the Eastern Front. Yet within two weeks the Allies had successfully swept the island. However, the Germans did manage to evacuate 50,000 men to mainland Italy.

Although a clear Allied victory, the operation was not without devastating mistakes. High winds dispersed paratroopers and gliders outside the intended drop areas. Poor communication and frayed nerves following Stuka dive-bombing attacks led Allied gunners to fire on their own transport ships, planes and paratroopers of the 504th Parachute Infantry Regiment.

The invasion of Sicily would be Phil's last battle. It would be analyzed and studied as a precursor of what to expect in less than a year along the beaches of Normandy. Lessons learned from the amphibious and airborne landings would be perfected and executed on June 6, 1944.

***

I was lucky to have been injured when I did. The really bad stuff, the heavy fighting, really began in Anzio. A lot of men from my unit were killed there or sent to German P.O.W. camps. I truly believe if I'd made it through Sicily I'd have been killed in Anzio, Cisterna or the D-Day invasion.

Back in Algiers I'm examined by the Doc. Says my arm is in a bad way and orders me to return to the U.S. I wasn't kicking. Waiting in a convalescent camp for shipment home, I decided to skip out and do some sightseeing. I made my way to the airport

---

*   During the Seventh Army's Sicilian campaign from July to September 1943, 21,482 soldiers were admitted to the hospital for malaria, while 17,535 were admitted for battle casualties.

and flew to Gibraltar. I walked the famous "Forty Steps" and wandered around Spain.

***

FORTY STEPS

Stars and Stripes, September 4, 1943

There's a place in Gibraltar, Britain's guardian of the west entrance of the Mediterranean, where lonesome Americans gather. And for my money, it is unique both in physical surrounding and the kind of hospitality that pervades it.

They call it "The Forty Steps" and it nestles right in The Rock, a thousand feet about the shimmering Mediterranean. From it you can see the Spanish city of Algeciras and if you squint hard enough, across the straits are the shores of Spanish Morocco in North Africa. You reach The Forty Steps only after clambering upward through a maze of winding alleys and twisting stairways that bring you out on Morello's Ramp.

The Forty Steps is actually the apartment of Corporal Jim Pace, former Miami Lawyer who now works in an Army finance office on "The Rock." Its name is derived from a street which leads onto the ramp. The good corporal started his self-appointed U.S.O. club four months ago with the idea that the few Americans at Gibraltar and those passing through ought to have a place to get together.

In the four rooms and patio you'll find an assorted collection of Yank soldiers, sailors, merchant seaman and airmen. Everyone is invited and when a colonel or major drops in, Corporal Pace greets him with his favorite salutation reserved for officers:

"Park your rank on the piano sir and come in and have a good time with

---

ABOVE LEFT Locals milling around at central train station in Palermo after the Allies captured the town. The two men in the background with Napoleonic-style hats are *Carabinieri*, Italian Military Police. Their name derived from *carabina*, the rifle they traditionally carried.
PHIL STERN

LEFT At the central train station in Palermo, Phil snaps a somber scene of an elderly man with his head held low, absorbed in his thoughts, shuffling between empty platforms, perhaps headed in the direction of Cefalu. A melancholy moment depicting the state of mind for many Sicilians at that time and place.
PHIL STERN

ABOVE Inside a hastily abandoned officer's quarters, Phil finds several items left behind: pictures of youngsters goose-stepping, a compass and, hanging properly in the latrine behind the house, a pristine picture of the Führer. Phil enlists the help of a couple of Rangers to pose with the portrait.
PHIL STERN

ABOVE LEFT A dozen Rangers loaded down with full combat gear wait for their buddy to refill the jeep's gas tank after breaking down on a hot Sicilian road.
PHIL STERN

LEFT When Allied forces seized Palermo Airport during Operation *Husky* in July 1943, it became a combat airfield for the 52nd Fighter Group. The Allies eventually handed over control of the airfield to the Co-belligerent Italian authorities when the Allied forces moved further north into Italy.
PHIL STERN

ABOVE A Ranger mans an antiaircraft gun at Palermo Airport. Having captured the ports of Agrigento and Porto Empedocle days earlier, Patton's Seventh Army entered the lightly defended northern capital on July 22, 1943. With the British moving towards Messina from the south, the Italians and Germans realized Sicily could no longer be defended and hastened a retreat from the island.

PHIL STERN

ABOVE LEFT American troops make their way to the towns of Comiso and Ragusa, where they meet up with British forces. By this time some 478,000 Allied troops had landed on Sicily, causing overwhelmed Germans to retreat to Messina. On July 25 Hitler ordered an official withdrawal of troops.

PHIL STERN

LEFT Major General George S. Patton, commander of the U.S. Seventh Army during the invasion of Sicily, congratulates Lieutenant Colonel William O. Darby and his troops for taking the Sicilian port town of Gela. After presenting Darby with the Distinguished Service Cross, Patton offered him command of an infantry combat team and a full colonelcy. Darby graciously declined, preferring to remain with his boys.

TIME INC.

Two native *Polizia* policeman pause long enough to be photographed by Phil. Previously under the authority of both the Defense and Interior Ministries, the police forces were transferred to the jurisdiction of the Allied Military Command after the invasion.
PHIL STERN

the boys. Visitors may drink and eat to their hearts' content in the definitely non-G.I. paradise." A tally is kept of their consumption in a little book designed especially for the purpose. At the end of the evening they pay just what the stuff cost, no more.

The apartment boasts a clubroom with a phone-radio and two pianos. A fixture of the place is Lola, the Spanish maid. She's tough. A sailor tried to make a pass at her the other day and she slapped him bowlegged. The wolves howl at a distance now.

Regulars at The Forty Steps are Corporal Curly Courtwrite of Los Angeles,

Sergeant Howard Cassier of Chelsea, Mass. and Captain Clifford Lord of San Francisco. They're stationed at Gibraltar and they'll tell you that The Steps have saved them from an early death of boredom. The night I was there a yarn-swapping circle included an Army major, some flyers, a man from the American Consul's office, some torpedoed merchant seaman and a sailor. In a quieter room some men were writing letters.

"I just started the place to have something to do and to keep from going 'rock-happy'," Pace told me. So if you ever get to The Rock and you're lonely for someone you can talk "American" with, remember that the latch is always out at The Forty Steps.

✳✳✳

I fly back to Tunis and catch a flight to Cairo where I spend a few hours taking in the sights. There are plenty of clubs for G.I.s on leave: the YMCA, Springbok and the Tipperary Tea Club. As I head back to Tunis an alert is issued. I hop along on a B-17 raid over Naples which turned out to be quite an adventure. It was incredible. Four hundred B-17 planes from NASAF (Northwest African Strategic Air Force) bombed the submarine base at Naples. The bombing went on for almost two hours. A bunch of ships in the harbor were sunk. The famous old church Santa Chiara and a hospital were totally destroyed. While General Patton and Montgomery were racing to see who would reach Messina first, I flew back to Tunis and boarded another plane for Palermo. I was there for three days. I stopped by the STARS AND STRIPES office to see the guys. Got some good photos of Bob Hope and his crew entertaining the troops. He sure does know how to make 'em laugh.

Back in Algiers the Stripers staff threw me a farewell party at the office. I'm going to miss those guys. We all tentatively shook hands and said "See you at home." My little tour around the Mediterranean was nearing the end. When I finally made my way back to the convalescent camp in Oran, I get bawled out by the captain. I give him a handful of postcards from my travels, which makes him happy.

CHAPTER 15

RECUPERATE AND RALLY

SEPTEMBER 1943

Sometime in September 1943, the U.S. Army treated me to a lovely cruise back home on the U.S.S. AMERICA, a former luxury cruise liner converted to an Army hospital ship. It felt real good sailing into the harbor. Almost like a dream. Docking on U.S. soil I was immediately sent to Tilton General Hospital at Fort Dix, New Jersey, to recuperate from those machine gun slugs courtesy of Herr Rommel's Panzers. They moved me to the Halloran General Hospital in Staten Island. My parents paid me a visit. Boy, was it good to see them.

I'm given a furlough from the hospital. On my way out, I pass a couple officers who I don't salute, and catch hell. I tell them my wounded hand hindered my ability to salute but gave it a try

In need of local heroes to hype, the War Department sends Staff Sergeant Stern on war-bond tours with celebrities such as Frank Sinatra and musician Artie Shaw. Phil retells war stories and hypes up his buddies, who were still over there fighting.
PHIL STERN ARCHIVES

THIS PAGE Assigned to photograph a *Stars and Stripes* event, Phil ran into some of his old reporter friends and a young Frank Sinatra. This photo (top) is thought to be the first he ever took of Ol' Blue Eyes. For the next five decades they would work together on several movie sets, Kennedy's Inauguration Gala and in the wee small hours at recording studios.
PHIL STERN

to keep the peace. "Where'd you learn to salute like that," one officer asked with disapproval. "Against the Hermann Göring Division," I replied.

I make my way to Fort Miles, Delaware. Uncle Sam thinks I'm some sort of war hero and decides to send me around the country touting war bonds. But first I pay a visit to a filmset in Astoria. Thought I'd see about some work.

✳✳✳

At the onset of the war, the U.S. Army acquired a defunct motion picture studio in Queens, New York. In February 1942, the studio officially became the Signal Corps Photographic Center, later named the Army Pictorial Center. Filmmakers and still photographers covered the war and produced countless training films and propaganda material there.

Not wasting any time, Phil contacted his former magazine editors. Having worked on a few filmsets before the war (*Citizen Kane*, *Sergeant York*), his real-life battle experience got him hired on war movies such as *Pork Chop Hill* and *To Hell and Back*.

Officially still in the Army, the War Department sent Staff Sergeant Stern and his Purple Heart to rallies with notable celebrities such as Artie Shaw and Frank Sinatra. "They had me flying all around the country," recalled Phil later in life. "Not a bad gig."

THE BULLY PULPIT

Despite working in the movies, Phil did not considered himself a cinephile. He preferred to watch newsreels about the war. However, two Soviet-themed films released in 1943 compelled Phil to write to his state senator about what he felt was "America's shameful response to a couple highly contentious Russian themed films while our allies were still fighting the war."

Mission to Moscow was the account of real-life Ambassador Joseph Davies. President Roosevelt sends him to Russia to learn about the Soviet system but he returns to America as an advocate of Stalinism. *The North Star* told the story of the resistance of Ukrainian villagers during the Nazi invasion in 1941. The film was also considered an unabashedly pro-Soviet propaganda film at the height of the war.

In November 1943, 24-year-old Stern wrote a letter to California Democratic Senator Sheridan Downey from the hospital where he was convalescing. The senator read his letter into the Congressional Record.

My first assignment for Stars and Stripes *was the invasion of Sicily. It was on the trek inland that I discovered something which should interest you, especially since the papers have often quoted you as speaking out for the unity of the United Nations abroad and democracy at home. We were ordered to set up our anti-tank guns on the fringes of Comiso Airport. We hopped into our half-track and headed for the Nazi airdrome. Halfway there, snipers opened up. All of us jumped off the vehicle, crawled on our stomachs toward an old house, which lodged the snipers. After a half hour of painstaking maneuvers we finally shot up the three Nazis in the house. One of the Germans had apparently fought in Russia, as in his pocket was a Nazi map of Russia. We also found a Nazi newspaper, "Eagle in the South." The unusual angle is that the sheet contained a blistering attack on the film, "Mission to Moscow."*

Now I'm on a 30-day convalescence furlough and I'm sore as hell to find many American newspapers and people swatting at the film "Mission to Moscow," in the same words and phrases used by that stained Nazi Wehrmacht newspaper I picked up outside of the Comiso Airport. It seems incredible that anyone here in the U.S.A. would use Nazi ammunition against an ally.

BLOWING OFF SOME STEAM

As the sun was setting in Union Square one fine May Day, in 1944, Phil happened upon one of those soapbox orators. Popping off about this and that, punctuating his wild statements with hatred. The recently discharged Sergeant Stern stepped up front and pulled out his Purple Heart medal from his pocket as he later recalled:

Do you know what this is?" he asked the speaker. "It's the Purple Heart," the orator replied. "Yes," said Phil. "I've got several slugs of shrapnel all over me fighting for punks like you!" Then he flattened him with a one–two. Spectators gathered around the soldier to congratulate him. "You all are worse!" Stern shouted. "You stood here letting him get away with it!" And he walked away.

V-Mail letter from Colonel Darby dated March 2, 1944 from somewhere in the Anzio beachhead. He wrote to ask Phil to send photos to his mother in Arkansas. Phil kept Darby's letter and made several copies. He scribbled these notes in the margins to Ranger Jim Altieri years later.

PHIL STERN

HI JIM = JUST RAN INTO THIS !
WOW — JUST LOOK AT ALL THE DETAILS HE GAVE !
"ANZIO" — "NEW COMMAND" ETC ETC
OF COURSE HE WAS HIS OWN CENSOR !
HOW SOON AFTER THIS LETTER WAS HE KILLED ?

I ALSO FOUND A CASHE OF FOTOS OF THE SICILIAN INVASION.

SOME REALLY RICH STUFF —

ALL THE BEST

LCE William O. Darby

(CENSOR'S STAMP)

No.

S/SGT PHIL STERN
802 W. 190 st
New York City
N.Y.

Colonel William O. Darby
Hqrs 179th Infantry
APO 45. % PM N.Y.
2 March '44

Somewhere in the
Anzio Beachhead

Dear Stern,

Enjoyed hearing from you — Much has happened since last writing. I now have a new job, and am in command of a Regiment ... note the new address ... I am two weeks ago — miss my gang — but I didn't have any chance in the matter.

Col .... was very pleased that you had sent the pictures to his wife. He is fine. Although we are now both members of your purple heart club. I now have a cluster — none of them were serious.*

I would be very happy if you would send any prints you have to my mother:
Her address: Mrs. P. W. Darby
41 Niland Hillcrest
Fort Smith, Arkansas
She would appreciate it very much — and so would I.
Thanks for writing and best of luck to you where ever your new job may take you.
Sincerely
Col Darby

V‑‑MAIL

* DEATH IS NOT SERIOUS ???

PHIL

NAZI RING

While fighting in Tunisia, Phil had taken a swastika ring off a dead Nazi officer. After returning home and becoming able to get around more freely, he decided to take the subway one day.

I was sitting on the Bronx Express reading a paper and my ring was smack up against the face of a middle-aged lady. She looked at the ring and at me and says: "You should be ashamed of yourself wearing a swastika and you, a boy in uniform. Phooey on that!" So I says to her, "Lady, I got it off a dead Nazi." And she says, "A dead Nazi?" and I say "Yes!" and then we were buddies. I got myself a friend for life.

COLONEL DARBY

In the spring of 1944 Phil received a letter from Colonel Darby, who was still based in Italy, requesting he send some photos to his mother in Arkansas.

Colonel William O. Darby
Ngrs 179th Infantry
APO 45, PM, N.Y.
2 March '44
Somewhere in the Anzio Beachhead

Dear Stern,

Enjoyed hearing from you. Much has happened since last writing. I now have a new job and I am in Command of a regiment. Note the new address. Miss my gang but I didn't have any claim in the matter.
Col. Dammer was very pleased that you had sent the pictures to his wife. He is fine although we are now both members of your Purple Heart club. I even have a cluster. None of them were serious. I would be very happy if you would send any prints you have to my mother. Her address:

Mrs. P.W. Darby
49 Hiland Hillcrest
Fort Smith, Arkansas

She would appreciate it very much and so would I. Thanks for writing and best of luck to you wherever your new job make take you.

Sincerely, Col. Darby

A few weeks later the two would meet up again at Camp Butner, not knowing it would be for the last time. Returning stateside in June 1944, Darby was assigned to the Operations Division of the War Department at the Pentagon. After spending a year in Washington strapped to a desk, Darby was finally reassigned, as assistant division commander, to the 10th Mountain Division then fighting the last vestiges of the German resistance in northern Italy.

On April 30, after a German counterattack on the town of Torbole in the Po Valley, Darby was one of two officers suddenly killed by a burst of German 88mm shells. A shell fragment the size of a dime pierced directly though Darby's heart. He was 34 years old. It was the same day Adolf Hitler committed suicide in his Führerbunker beneath the Reich Chancellery in Berlin and two days after Mussolini and his mistress were slain and hanged by Italian partisans in Milan. On May 2 German forces in Italy surrendered unconditionally at noon. On May 15, 1945 President Truman posthumously promoted Darby to the rank of brigadier general.

By the time of Colonel Darby's tragic death in the final days of World War II, Phil's own military career was formally over. On May 2, 1944, Phil was officially given a medical discharge from the service at Fort Totten, a United States Army installation in the New York City borough of Queens.

LIFE

RUSSIA'S
GENERALS

JULY 31, 1944 **10** CENTS
YEARLY SUBSCRIPTION $4.50

CHAPTER 16

POST WAR, RECOLLECTIONS AND REMINISCENCES

REUNION WITH THE RANGERS

In the days leading up to the D-Day invasion on the beaches of Normandy, France, *Life Magazine* handed Phil his first major assignment as a veteran. Teaming up with war correspondent and writer John Hersey, Phil traveled to Camp Butner in Durham, North Carolina, to photograph what remained of his fellow Rangers for a five-page photo spread.

While Phil was recuperating stateside after reinjuring old wounds and collecting some new ones, the rest of the Rangers were fighting their way through the most brutal battles of the Italian Campaign. Decimated during the disastrous battles of Anzio and Cisterna, his friends were either gravely wounded, killed in action, sent to P.O.W. camps or transferred to other units. In the end, only six of 760 men who infiltrated to Cisterna made their way back to Allied lines. The 1st, 3rd and 4th Ranger, Battalions were subsequently disbanded. Of the original 1,500 Rangers, only 199 returned home.

General Georgy Zhukov, the most highly decorated Russian commander, graced the cover of the July 31, 1944, issue of *Life* magazine. It also featured the story of the Rangers' reunion at Camp Butner. A dozen of the most victorious Russian generals of the Red Army at the time were also profiled.

TIME INC.; PHOTOGRAPH BY GREGORY WEIL, PUBLIC DOMAIN

The main photo spread in the issue was an extreme wide shot displaying the devastating loss of Darby's Rangers. Of the original Rangers, 97 survivors stand in formation in the foreground. Behind them are three Army battalions – 1,500 troops represent the original strength of the 1st Ranger Battalion.
PHIL STERN

It was a frantic but welcome couple of days for Phil, shooting photos of buddies he hadn't seen since Sicily. The centerpiece of the essay was a panorama shot comparing the original number of Rangers to the remaining men that were still standing. Phil assembled and lined up 97 Rangers. Behind them stood soldiers representing their original strength of about 1,500. Phil was having a field day. It was the first chance he had to boss a whole rank of officers around. In order to get his wide shot he climbed up a shaky ladder to the roof of an adjacent building. After a couple of tries he finally got his shot.

Lieutenant Chuck Shunstrom, "The Wild Man of Anzio," surprised everyone when he unexpectedly showed up with his wife and 22-month-old daughter. Captured by the Nazis in Cisterna, he escaped from the P.O.W. Stalag II-B camp in northern Germany. After traveling 600 miles through snow-filled mountains, he eventually made it to the Allied lines. He was put on a plane in Gibraltar, landing a day later at LaGuardia Field in Queens, New York. Colonel Darby later made an appearance on June 20 to commemorate the second anniversary of the Rangers with 22,000 people in attendance. A party with family members was held but emotions were mixed as many Rangers were still fighting in Europe, being held captive or missing in action.

The local press in Durham, North Carolina, was in full force to welcome the Rangers home. Obligingly, they shared their wartime escapades with reporters. At times it was solemn. Out of action for several months while his buddies were still fighting, Phil was excited to catch up with everyone. Finding himself in a large group of Rangers they'd start talking and reminiscing. Eventually he'd ask about some of the guys. The answer was almost always the same: "he's gone," or "he didn't make it."

Phil bumped into Captain Richard D. Hardenbrook, a strong, unassuming medical officer assigned to the Rangers. The Rochester, New York, man recalled the bravery of the Rangers.

> *The wounded would insist the doctor attend to other men who appeared in worse off condition. What caused a great deal of trouble was the men going AWOL from the hospital every time they heard the Rangers were leaving for combat. They were afraid the outfit would leave without them. Anxious to get back into action, these men felt it was an honor to belong to the Rangers and didn't want to miss a bit of the action.*

Stories were retold of those who had lived and died in Sicily, Salerno, Anzio and Cisterna. To cope, they covered them with humor. Many a funny incident kept them "blowing their tops." Phil recounted a strange tale of the monkey and the soldier for the press:

> *Taking shelter in a foxhole to escape severe shelling, a G.I. whose name escapes me was joined by a small monkey common to North Africa. The frightened monkey clung to the soldier in terror while the soldier caressed the little animal and soothed his nerves. After the shelling the poor little monkey refused to leave the soldier and they became inseparable companions. When it came time for the soldier to return to the U.S. on the rotation plan, he refused to leave without the monkey. The little creature was given a complete physical, tetanus and typhoid shots, made a T-5 and given a service record. When they arrived in the U.S. an official told him it was against regulations to bring an animal back to the States. The soldier showed his papers and proceeded on his way.*

Writer John Hersey interviews Rangers for the *Life* magazine essay. The war correspondent served in Italy, accompanying Allied troops during the invasion of Sicily. He went on to be a successful author, beginning with the 1945 Pulitzer Prize-winning novel *A Bell for Adano*.
PHIL STERN

"Being shock troops got in their blood," remarked Sergeant Mark Morris, a reporter for *Yank*. "There was just one thing about that kind of fighting. By damn, it gave you a thrill," said one Ranger, who wished to remain anonymous. "We never had to ask questions about who was out front; we just started shooting. Hell, nobody wants to get killed and I was plenty scared sometimes – but it gave you a thrill, the way we fought." One Irish first sergeant told of the other side of the coin. "It wasn't always fun. Sometimes, when you were under it, that Jerry artillery made you want to cry."

Even from when the unit was formed the Rangers had not had it easy. Indeed, the Rangers suffered more casualties training in Scotland than they did on their first African landing. "We maneuvered with live ammunition. There were accidents, too. They had us out in a place one time that wasn't entirely cleared of old land mines they'd put there when the invasion was expected. Two of our boys jumped a barbed wire fence and landed right on top of a mine. We were picking them up two days later. Another guy fell off a cliff and broke practically every bone in his body."

"The Rangers have great pride in their unit," wrote Morris. "They are certain they were the best fighters in the world. If you should be so brave as to ask a Ranger what was so great about his outfit he'd either knock you down or say something similar to what Sergeant George H. Creed, a former coal miner from West Virginia, stated: 'I wouldn't take 1,000 bucks to get out of the outfit and I wouldn't take $3,000 to get in another just like it.'"

The town hall in Licata was the inspiration for John Hersey's novel *A Bell for Adano*. Mussolini ordered the cherished bell removed and melted down for weapons and ammunition. An empty space marks where the 700-year-old bell rang out daily. Phil took this picture in Sicily, July 1942.
PHIL STERN

"It's hard to explain," said Phil. "But life is fuller for me now. Those little disappointments I had before the war I welcome now. It's a part of life. Those things like good friends, good food and a comfortable bed are not to be taken for granted. I slept on rocky ground, haven't eaten for long periods of time and saw good friends die. I can't forget that too easily."

Corporal J. Hull Wilson described Phil as "a husky, handsome bruiser of a guy. Just a kid from Brooklyn who felt America had given him a birthright worth risking his life for. Often referred to as 'the kid who shoots those super-duper pictures for *Life Magazine*' and 'one of America's foremost news cameramen,' after the war Phil was always happiest when someone points to him and says, 'That's Phil Stern, of the 1st Ranger Battalion.'"

FELLOW WAR CORRESPONDENTS

JOHN HERSEY

While Phil was happily in charge ordering everyone around the base as they posed for photos, writer John Hersey was busy interviewing men for the *Life* essay. The war correspondent for *Time* magazine served in Italy during the war, accompanied Allied troops during the invasion of Sicily and survived four airplane crashes. Hersey would go on to become a successful author, beginning with his 1945 Pulitzer Prize-winning novel *A Bell for Adano*, based on the real Sicilian coastal port town of Licata, the beach where Phil came ashore during the Sicilian invasion. In Hersey's novel the main character is an Italian-American named Major Victor Joppo, based on U.S. Army Major Frank E. Toscani. As the temporary American military governor of the town of Licata during occupation, Joppo's mission was to bring justice to the town after years of Nazi occupation and Benito Mussolini's Fascist regime. He soon learned from the townspeople about a story of a cherished 700-year-old church bell that was removed and melted down for weapons by *Il Duce*. A replacement bell was eventually found, donated by the destroyer U.S.S. *Corelli*.

Hersey continued to cover the fighting in Europe and Asia. His reportage on the aftermath of the atomic bomb dropped over Hiroshima in 1945 became the subject of his second book, *Hiroshima*.

After first meeting at Camp Butner, the two war reporters would keep in touch over the years until Hersey's passing in 1993.

SERGEANT PETE PARIS

Learning of the death of a fellow photographer during the D-Day landings, Phil penned this letter to *Yank Magazine*:

Dear Yank:

I've just read in the newspapers about Sergeant Pete Paris, your Yank *staff photographer, getting killed in action during the D-Day landings in Normandy. The news hit me like a shell burst. I was a combat photographer in Sicily and Tunisia with the 1st Ranger Battalion and I don't think I ever went up into a hot spot during those campaigns without finding Pete and his camera in the middle of things. I remember him at Dernaia, Fériana, Kasserine, Gafsa and Licata, making sure that* Yank *readers had close-up pictures of the doggies in action.*

Besides being a great war photographer, Pete was a great friend of the guys in every outfit that had him along. A grimy-faced machine gunner from the 18th Infantry told me once at El Guettar: "That crazy bastard Paris will do anything to get a good action picture but he's got guts and he is okay for my dough."

When a guy is killed the papers write about how good he was and what he achieved. The thousands of G.I.s who knew Pete Paris in Africa, Sicily and the ETO won't need to read any such obituaries about him. They could write one themselves with no trouble at all.

Ex-Sgt. PHIL STERN
New York, N.Y.

NOËL THE COWARD

In 1943 with the war still raging in Europe, Noël Coward, a well-to-do English playwright and British Intelligence officer, caught the ire of Phil, a couple dozen G.I.s and nearly the entire borough of Brooklyn. The flamboyant Coward conducted the British equivalent of a United Service Organizations (U.S.O.) tour to entertain troops in North Africa and a three-month tour of hospitals filled with wounded British and American soldiers from July to October 1943. His experiences were published in his *Middle East Diary*. Coward made several statements that offended more than a few Americans. One comment in particular caused a huge commotion: "I was less impressed by some of the mournful little Brooklyn boys lying there in tears amid the alien corn with nothing worse than a bullet wound in the leg or a fractured arm." This did not sit well with Phil and other Brooklynites so he crafted a fiery retort to the playwright via the *San Francisco Chronicle*.

BROOKLYN BOY BREAKS WITH MR. NOEL COWARD
It Ain't Epigrams the Wild-Eyed Fighter Wants to Trade, Either
Mr. Phil Stern, the gentleman from Brooklyn who stops Nazi bullets and snaps pictures with equal éclat, yesterday severed diplomatic relations with Mr. Noël Coward, the gentleman from London. Tieless and with a wild glint in his eye, Stern stormed into The Chronicle *yesterday to answer Coward's controversial comments on the subject of "mournful little Brooklyn boys" in military hospitals.*

No dodger, although he hails from Flatbush, Stern entered the Army as a Signal Corps photographer and then transferred to Colonel William "Wild Bill" Darby's 1st Ranger Battalion. Out of 1500 men who comprised this group, only 177 are still alive.

"Now let me get this straight," announced Stern. "This character Coward said, 'I was less impressed by some of the mournful little Brooklyn boys lying there in tears amidst the alien corn with nothing worse than a bullet wound in the leg or a fractured arm.' I met Coward once in one of those fancy private clubs in London when I was

with the Signal Corps. He was immaculately dressed with a big cocktail glass in his hand. He was a real bon vivant making smart cracks and very much against the war. As a matter of fact this Coward knows more about cocktails in his gizzard than about bullet wounds in the leg. Now you take Colonel Darby's original outfit for example. The ones who are alive, I mean. At least 11 of them that I knew personally are from Brooklyn. In fact, about everybody I ever met over there came either from Brooklyn or Texas. For instance, there was Sergeant Carlo Contreas, who was Colonel Darby's jeep driver and personal Tommy gunner. We were advancing through Sicily when we came into a little town. Colonel Darby says: 'Contreas, knock out that pill box ahead of us.' Contreas takes his Tommy gun and moves forward then pauses for a minute. The Colonel yelled, 'What's the matter Contreas, are you yellow?'

'No Sir. I ain't scared,' Contreas mumbled on. 'I'm just shaking with patriotism.' So Contreas went ahead and knocked out the pill box all by himself and then he and the Colonel captured the town behind it."

That was just one "mournful little Brooklyn Boy" whose exploits Stern recalled. Wearer of the Purple Heart medal, Stern waxed very eloquent on the subject of little Brooklyn boys who went through the hell of Anzio, Salerno and Sicily without batting an eye. He also spoke glowingly about all the Englishmen he had ever met.

"They were warm and friendly and understanding," he said. "They didn't care whether we came from Brooklyn or Flagstaff and they didn't care anything about our race or our religion. We were American soldiers and that was enough for all of them except this character, Coward."

Stern, who once ordered a German officer to surrender in his best Brooklyn Yiddish, continued his diatribe by declaring war on the British playwright.

"I will consider it a great privilege to knock his teeth in," he said. "Also, I think his plays stink."

Meanwhile, in Paris, Coward hedged on the remark that yesterday aroused the whole of Brooklyn to such a pitch of fury that city officials are asking the playwright henceforth be denied entry to the United States.

"Did I mention Brooklyn troops at all?" Coward asked a United Press representative. "I have no recollection of the diary entry and I do not recall any groups which could be described as Brooklyn."

The much-mooted paragraph is included in Coward's latest book, Middle East

In 1951 Phil risked his life shooting the cover of *Ebony Magazine*. It featured the U.S. Air Force's first African-American experimental test pilot, Lieutenant John Whitehead. During the war he had trained with the Tuskegee Airmen.
PHIL STERN

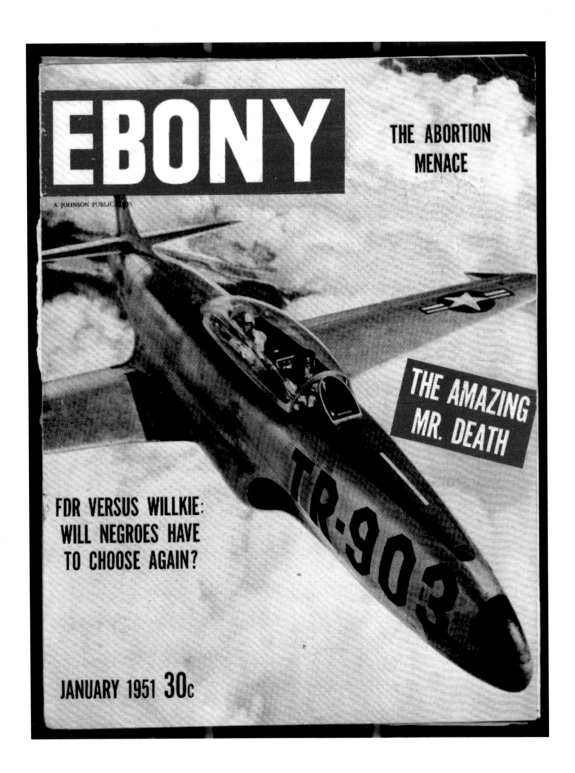

Diary. *Brooklynites are asking it be banned in New York City. After protests from the* New York Times *and the* Washington Post, *the Foreign Office urged Coward not to visit the United States in January 1945.*

A NEW LIFE

"Married? No, but I'll certainly be a dream boy for some girl," Phil stated on his return home. "A hundred dollars a month for life from the government besides what I can earn. Plus I can get a house and lot in Los Angeles for practically nothing."

A few days before the bomb was dropped on Hiroshima in 1945, Phil did indeed get married, to the glamorous John Robert Powers model, Rosemae Lindou. Together they had four children: Phillip ("Flip"), Lata, Peter and Tom. Sadly, two of his children preceded him in death. His eldest son Flip died in a plane crash at Van Nuys Airport in 1969 and Lata, a film producer who worked on *Jurassic Park*, *Star Wars – Return of the Jedi* and *Indiana Jones and the Last Crusade*, died from complications of pancreatic cancer in 2003.

In addition to the Hollywood scene, Phil worked as a set photographer on over 100 movies, and photographed 60 jazz album covers and singers for American jazz music impresario Norman Granz's Pablo and Verve record labels. In between these gigs he'd cover social and political issues, such as the stealthy shot he got of Edith Irby, the first black student to attend the University of Arkansas School of Medicine on her first day of class in September 1948.

One of his most daring assignments had Phil precariously hanging from a B-25 bomber. The 1951 cover of *Ebony Magazine* featured the United States Air Force's first African-American experimental test pilot, Lieutenant John Whitehead, commonly referred to as "Mr. Death" – not because of his daring skills in soaring through the stratosphere, but because of his gaunt, shrunken face and skeleton-like frame. Phil's remarkable cover shot of Mr. Death's jet was taken from 12,500 feet from the tail of a B-25 bomber. The attached rear casing was removed so he could extend the camera beyond the plane. Phil was held into his position by a rope. It was just the kind of daring assignment that he liked, reminding him of his war service and time with the Rangers, before life was more comfortable.

RIGHT In 1945, a few days before the end of the war with Japan, Phil married model Rosemae Lindou in Los Angeles City Hall. They had four children together before a divorce in the late 1960s. Phil never remarried.
PHIL STERN ARCHIVES

CHAPTER 17

THE GOLDEN AGE

The 1950s was a golden age for Hollywood and a gold mine for Phil. The snapper worked nonstop for top celebrity magazines and film studios. "I was hired to do photographic coverage with a different point of view than staff photographers who shot the highly glamorized celebrity portraits. I caught them in unguarded moments. That's what the studio and magazines were looking for at the time."

On occasion he'd bump into a star or two and hit it off, as was the case when he met James Dean, John Wayne, Humphrey Bogart and Frank Sinatra.

THE DUKE

During his decades-long career John Wayne appeared in several World War II films such as *The Sands of Iwo Jima* and *The Longest Day*. Unlike other male stars of the day (such as Jimmy Stewart, Henry Fonda and Clark Gable), Wayne had not

At the Shrine Auditorium in Los Angeles for a children's benefit in 1953, Marilyn Monroe was as usual surrounded by a gaggle of photographers. Phil waited for the right moment as she was going over her lines backstage. "My picture of her was a fluke," recalled Phil. "Dozens of flashes were going off. Suddenly she twitched and I clicked the shutter. I got my shot."
PHIL STERN

served. He received a 3-A deferment from the draft for family dependency. His longtime collaborator and director John Ford, a commander in the U.S. Navy, berated him to "get into it."

"Wayne and I were poster boys for *The Odd Couple*," said Phil, who first worked with "The Duke" in the 1950s when the Red Scare of the McCarthyism was at its peak. "We were polar opposites when it came to politics. He was ultra-right wing conservative and I was ultra-left. He was a mixed bag, like all of us. He had his tender, warm, loving moments, but he was also a son of a bitch." Stern recalled an incident where he witnessed Wayne firing a set photographer on the spot. "He was very tenacious about protecting his identity as a western, macho he-man. He would not allow anyone to make fun of that except himself. I had many opportunities to get some great photographs of him in compromising positions. One in particular had him sitting on a barrel attached to a rope, while two grips on each side shook it to appear like he's riding a horse. As much as I wanted to take that picture I knew he would be irate and I needed to protect my livelihood."

In the 1960s, Phil and Wayne caroused their way through Europe, Africa and Mexico while working on various films such as *True Grit*, *El Dorado* and *The Alamo*. "For reasons I don't understand he felt comfortable with me around and we developed a certain amount of intimacy. Politically and socially he was 140 degrees to the right of Genghis Khan. I was oppositely inclined. Whenever we got loaded we'd have heated arguments about politics. He'd call me a bomb-throwing Bolshevik and I would retort by calling him a Neanderthal fucking fascist. It was a love-hate thing."

AUDIE MURPHY

By the time Audie Leon Murphy was 21, he'd become the most decorated soldier of World War II. During his three years of active service, First Lieutenant Murphy received every decoration of valor that the United States had to offer, some of them more than once. His medals included five decorations from France and Belgium. Among his 33 awards and decorations was the prestigious Medal of Honor, the highest military award for bravery that can be given to any individual in the United States of America.

Phil and John Wayne, "The Duke," were polar opposites in terms of politics. But their differences were all in good humor and they often took family vacations together.
PHIL STERN

"Although Audie's wartime travels and mine covered some of the same terrain in North Africa and Sicily, we never met until after the war when he got a studio contract," recounted Phil. "We became good friends. Audie was essentially an iconoclastic, to put it mildly. His attitude about movies was this; he avoided Hollywood social life as much as possible. He said to me once, 'Phil, if I knew another way in another place in which I could make the kind of money I make in Hollywood with this film business, I would run there. But this is unbeatable.' He was an interesting guy. When he finished a movie, he disappeared. He didn't do any of the Hollywood numbers that we're familiar with. There was a guy that he grew up with in Texas – I think they were school chums – a guy with the improbable name of Terwillager. I don't remember his first name, but with a name like Terwillager, a first name would dilute it. They were inseparable. His big joy was taking off with his Texas chum to go hunting and deep-sea fishing together. Terwillager was a cowhand, but Audie used him as his stand-in and stunt double.

At that time, I was married with four children and a house in the San Fernando Valley. From time to time Audie and Terwillager would stop by in a pickup truck at Chez Moi with large quantities of their catch. It could be anything from venison, wild pig, tuna, bonito or yellowtail. On the first occasion, he brought big sacks of tuna and barracuda. My family ate this stuff for weeks. It was fabulous food. The next time he came, he brought a wild pig they hunted on Catalina Island – which was delicious stuff. And another time it was deer meat, which I had never had, but my ex-wife had a fabulous recipe for cooking venison and I got to like it. We had to buy a big freezer because whenever he came by with that pickup truck, we had meat for months. He picked people that had a lot of kids which I thought was so thoughtful of him. 'Hey Phil, you got a lot of mouths to feed,' he once said. Those mouths ate 'Murphy Specials' very happily for a long time."

ABOVE LEFT Phil and Audie Murphy on the set of *The Unforgiven*. Considered the most decorated U.S. soldier of World War II, Murphy received the Medal of Honor for valor for single-handedly holding off an entire company of German soldiers for an hour at the Colmar Pocket in France in January 1945, then leading a successful counterattack while wounded and out of ammunition.
MARGARET HERRICK LIBRARY

LEFT James Dean had a fascination with photography. He and Phil would often discuss the finer principles of picture-taking over coffee at the infamous Schwab's drugstore. Dean turned the tables on Phil, having him pose on his Triumph motorcycle in 1955.
JAMES DEAN

This snap of James Dean is one of Phil's most famous and purchased photographs. Phil stated several times that he had nothing to do with this shot. No direction or cajoling. "He just came in and started posing with his sweater. It was a whimsical statement of his own volition and I'm eternally thankful for it."

PHIL STERN

WAR MOVIES

At Goldwyn Studios while they were making Guys and Dolls, *I had a flurry of activity for books and magazines who were doing stories related to World War II. I had an unusual number of calls for material for those books and articles. The Goldwyn Production office gave me permission to carve out an area of Stage 4 where* Guys and Dolls *was being shot. It was a huge stage and there was an area they didn't need so they let me partition it off. I brought in hundreds of prints to organize and caption to prepare for the various editorial queries I had for that material. I'd tack the prints up on a Celotex wall and make my notes on them. I had a whole wall and a half filled with those prints.*

While working on them one day, an old-time set decorator named Robert Boyle accidentally barged into my area. He started looking at the prints on the wall. "Hey Phil! These are rather interesting. Don't tell me, let me guess … you made those on an MGM battleground." I said, "No, I didn't." He went on, "Did you make them on Pork Chop Hill, *the film that Gregory Peck did about the Korean*

ABOVE While Phil preferred classical music he photographed 60 album covers for jazz music impresario Norman Granz's Pablo and Verve record labels. They featured Louis Armstrong, Ella Fitzgerald, Billie Holiday, Nat King Cole, Stan Getz, Dizzy Gillespie and Vladimir Horowitz.
PHIL STERN

ABOVE RIGHT Ella Fitzgerald and Louis Armstrong in the studio. The jazz legends recorded 11 ballads for the album *Ella and Louis* in 1956 and were photographed during the sessions by Phil.
PHIL STERN

War?" I said, "No, none of them." He said, "Jesus, Phil, what show did you make those on?" I said, "World War II." He paused, a bit embarrassed, and said, "I'm so Hollywood oriented. I've got to get out of Hollywood. I can't take it anymore."

JAMES DEAN

Phil almost became the man that killed James Dean. On the day they first met in May 1955, during the early morning hours, Phil was cruising west on Sunset Boulevard near Crescent Heights Boulevard in Hollywood on his way to *Life*'s editorial offices on the Sunset Strip:

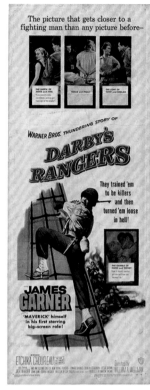

ABOVE Nearly 15 years after the end of the war, in 1957, Phil and Jim Altieri, author of *The Spearheaders* and *Darby's Rangers*, discuss a shot in front of a bunker on the Warner Brothers back lot. Both men were hired as advisors and actors.
PHIL STERN / MARGARET HERRICK LIBRARY

ABOVE RIGHT *"They trained 'em to be killers and then turned 'em loose in hell!"* read the tagline on the movie poster for *Darby's Rangers* in 1958. In the year since filming ended, James Garner had shot to celebrity status on TV in *Maverick*. The studio smartly hyped their new star on the poster: *"'Maverick' himself in his first starring big-screen role!"*
WARNER BROTHERS

This crazy guy on a motorcycle comes barreling down Laurel Canyon through a red light and nearly runs into my car. We both careened through the intersection. I was fuming. After screaming some explicatives out the window I pulled over to see if he was ok. As he got up off the ground he had a dopey grin on his face. He told me his name was James Dean. I didn't know who he was. Looking back now I could have been the guy famous for running over James Dean. We ended up having a two-hour breakfast at Schwab's drugstore.

Although Phil was a decade older than Dean, the two hit it off: "I was a Jewish kid from New York, he was a Midwestern eccentric. At the time I was working on the Goldwyn lot on *Guys and Dolls*, so I invited Dean to the set for lunch. I told him Marlon Brando would be there."

A bespectacled Dean showed up, Brando didn't. However that day was frozen in time when Phil shot two of his most iconic pictures of the tragic star. One of Dean casually lounging on a director's chair with his feet propped up on a ladder, and a playful shot with just his wild hair and blue eyes peering out of a black turtleneck sweater.

"Later I did a photo shoot of Jimmy for *Photoplay Magazine*. He and his cronies would hang out till late night at Googies Coffee Shop drinking coffee and eating apple pie. Jimmy was always at the center of attention."

Dean had a fascination with photography so he turned the camera on Phil one day outside of Googies, posing the snapper on his Triumph motorcycle.

Four months later, on September 30, 1955, the 24-year-old heartthrob from Indiana died tragically in a fiery car accident on his way to a race near Cholame, California.

DARBY'S RANGERS: THE MOVIE

Ranger James Altieri's biographical account of *Darby's Rangers* hit the big screen on February 12, 1958. Phil was hired as a set photographer and technical advisor, along with Altieri and Colonel Roy Murray. Phil and Roy were also cast as supporting actors.

Like many films, drama and big egos caused trouble behind the scenes. Tension had been festering between Oscar-winning director William Wellman and Warner Brothers boss Jack Warner from their previous collaboration on the film *Lafayette Escadrille*, based on Wellman's exploits during World War I. The director of the first Academy Award for Best Picture for *Wings* had served with the French Lafayette Flying Corps as a fighter pilot. It was said he directed "like a general trying to break out of a beachhead."

With a budget of just under one million dollars, filming commenced on the soundstages of Warner Brothers' back lot where Wellman's other war films, *The Story of G.I. Joe* and *Battleground*, were filmed.

Warner cast Charlton Heston for the role of Darby, allowing Wellman to hire the rest of the cast. Wellman brought in actors who had been released from the studio's contract system and cast them. The thespians were put through two weeks' basic training and drill instruction in order to feel and act like real soldiers. Warner's deal with Heston fell apart just before filming was set to start on April 22, 1957. Wellman was forced to delay the start until a star actor was signed. Tired of waiting, Wellman had his actors line up, announcing, "There's been a casting problem for the lead. Everyone move up one part." Fledgling actor James Garner stepped up suddenly realizing, "If I move up I'm Darby, the lead!" and so a Hollywood star was born, with Phil there to witness the start of another famous career.

THE DEVIL AT 4 O'CLOCK

Of all the celebrities Phil rubbed elbows with, his relationship with Frank Sinatra was the longest and most genial, spanning six decades, a couple of wives, bad films, late night studio sessions and a presidential bash. However Phil would tell you he wasn't a part of Sinatra's inner circle but "For some reason he trusted me." Phil never wanted to be what we'd now called a poser or hanger-on. He had a job to do. Indeed, the very first shot he took of Ol' Blue Eyes was of a baby-faced young bobby sox crooner dressed to the nines with a polka dot bow tie. Because he had a perforated eardrum from birth Sinatra was disqualified as 4-F during the war. He took a lot of guff but did his part performing at the Hollywood Canteen and U.S.O. overseas.

In 1960 Phil was on location with Frank on the Hawaiian Island of Maui. They were filming *The Devil at 4 O'Clock*, starring Sinatra and Spencer Tracy, who played an eccentric priest marooned on a volcanic island in the South Seas. Frank and his brother-in-law, Peter Lawford, had been campaigning for Senator John Kennedy all around the islands. Both Phil and Frank were still on set when they learned J.F.K. had won the election. Sinatra was thrilled when Kennedy showed his appreciation for his support by asking him to stage the Inaugural Gala. As

TOP LEFT Phil pictured on set with director William Wellman. Wellman's directing style was once described as "a general trying to break out of a beachhead." His clashes with Warner Brothers President Jack Warner were notorious. Their bickering continued with even more fury during the filming. Wellman retired from show business after *Darby's Rangers* wrapped.
MARGARET HERRICK LIBRARY

TOP RIGHT Rangers Reunite – no longer dodging real bullets and bombs, three original Darby's Rangers, Jim Altieri, Phil Stern and Roy Murray, Jr. reunite on the set of the film version of *Darby's Rangers*. The movie did fairly well at the box office despite mediocre reviews from the original Rangers.
MARGARET HERRICK LIBRARY

RIGHT James Garner as Colonel Darby looks on as the real Colonel Roy Murray, playing himself, pins a Purple Heart Medal on Phil for being wounded by shrapnel from Rommel's Panzers during the Battle of El Guettar.
WARNER BROTHERS

soon as Phil heard the news, he wanted in on the action. "I knew it would be a historic occasion so I wrote a note to Frank on a file card and left it in his dressing room." His pitch came in the guise of an enamored schoolboy's note:

```
FRANK:

I WANT THE JOB OF BEING RESIDENT PHOTOG WHEN YOU
PREP AND PUT ON THE JFK INAUGURAL GALA.

FOR YOUR CONVENIENCE JUST CHECK THE APPROPRIATE
BOX BELOW:
                                        Phil Stern


YES. [ ]


I'LL THINK ABOUT IT [ ]

FUCK OFF. [ ]
```

He got the gig. Phil would be the exclusive resident paparazzo of President John F. Kennedy's Inaugural Gala. Despite a massive snowstorm blanketing the nation's capital, the star-studded bash went on without a hitch. The night was filled with Hollywood glamour and the aura of a bright, promising future.

One of Phil's most iconic shots from that night was off the cuff. "At the Washington D.C. Statler Hilton post-inaugural party, the Latin American Room was lit entirely by candlelight," Phil later recalled. Frank had asked him not to use flashes. President Kennedy sat down next to Sinatra, who lit up a cigarette for him. Phil quickly took a shot, capturing a historic moment. It would be the last time a sitting president was photographed smoking. Unbeknownst to either man, it would be the last time the two ever spoke or saw one another again.

Shortly after the gala, Frank and Phil worked tirelessly for weeks in Phil's Van Nuys, California, home designing personalized, spiral-bound photo albums for each of the 30 entertainers, the President and the First Lady.

ABOVE Sinatra gave Phil the gig as the official photographer of J.F.K.'s Inaugural Gala. He snapped
this photo of Sinatra casually lighting Kennedy's cigarette.
PHIL STERN

NEXT PAGES First Lady Jacqueline Kennedy and President John Fitzgerald Kennedy make their
way down Pennsylvania Avenue after the President was sworn in on January 20, 1961. The evening
prior Washington D.C. was buried under more than eight inches of heavy, wet snow, threatening
the inauguration ceremony, but enthusiastic workers with shovels and flamethrowers worked until
the small hours to help celebrate the historic day.
PHIL STERN

CHAPTER 18

LATER LIFE, 1980–2014

As the 1980s began, Phil slowed down as he headed into his sixties. Years of smoking had taken its toll. He would suffer from emphysema for the rest of his life, his oxygen tank always by his side.

"My career, my hands-on trade of photography, stopped in the early 1980s," he lamented. Still lively, he worked on recycling his youth by mining his archives for commercial purposes: books, exhibits, postcards and other paraphernalia. It meant long hours cataloging mountains of material from six decades then canning them for the digital world. "I found the quality amazing, the imagery that comes from the computer. Initially, I resisted it like all old guys do."

Over the years, filmmakers, documentarians and authors came calling, looking to use Phil's photos in their projects. Advertisers came knocking as well. The GAP's 1993 Khakis campaign featured Phil's photos of John Wayne and Sammy Davis Jr.

During his return visit to Sicily in 2013, Phil went back to all the places he had photographed in his youth. Interviewed for a documentary, Phil is seated in front of the Citadel, an ancient castle in the town of Butera. During the invasion of Sicily, Rangers, led by Captain Chuck Shunstrom, successfully assaulted the fortress, which perched on a 4,000-foot hill.
HECTOR SANDOVAL

James Dean casually lounging in a director's chair, his Jack Pursell sneakers perched on a ladder while on the set of *Guys and Dolls*, became a lucrative ad campaign for Converse shoes, earning Phil – as he phrased it – a nice chunk of change.

Realizing his prints were now considered fine art he began selling and exhibiting his photographs through Fahey/Klein Gallery in Los Angeles and Staley-Wise Gallery in New York. His work was displayed across the country and around the world in Milan, Sicily, New York City, Philadelphia and San Francisco.

Seeking out his images of a bygone era, celebrities and collectors such as Madonna, Steven Spielberg, Gary Oldham and Michael Jackson would come knocking at his Hollywood bungalow right across the street from Paramount studios.

REUNIONS

Phil flew to Scotland in 1991 for "The Last Hurrah," the 50th anniversary of the formation of the Rangers, accompanied by a diminishing group of Rangers. They returned to the training grounds where it all began, visiting Achnacarry Castle and the Commando Memorial at Spean Bridge. Their beloved Father Basil, the Rangers chaplain who had traveled with them to North Africa, was there to welcome his old American friends and lead the prayers, as he had done so long ago.

In the summer of 2013, Phil was the guest of honor for the ten-day celebration in Sicily of the 70th anniversary of Operation *Husky*. It was a whirlwind of nonstop activities. Two exhibitions showcased Phil's photographs, documentaries were filmed, and marching bands filled the streets. The 93-year-old, pushing his walker everywhere he went, was energized and surprised by the large crowds that showed up at the events, which included speaking engagements with photography students at the Catania Art School and U.S. Navy cadets at nearby U.S. Naval Air Station Sigonella. An emotional trip back to the Licata

RIGHT TOP Colonel William Darby's 1st Ranger Battalion on a grueling speed march during training with British Commandos at Achnacarry, Scotland, July 1942.
PHIL STERN

RIGHT 1991: They may not be as fast as they once were, and the number has dwindled considerably, but in the Ranger and Commando spirit a determined few reenact the 1942 speed march on the same exact spot 50 years later. Note the familiar white farmhouse in the background, half hidden by trees and still-standing fences.
PHIL STERN

War photographers (left to right): Carl Mydans, who photographed General Douglas MacArthur wading ashore on his triumphant return to the Philippines; Eddie Adams, the 1969 Pulitzer Prize winner for his photograph of South Vietnam police chief General Nguyen Ngoc Loan executing a Viet Cong prisoner on a Saigon street; German photojournalist Hilmar Pabel; Phil Stern; Nick Ut, the 1972 Pulitzer Prize winner for his photo of "The Napalm Girl" during the Vietnam War; and Joe Rosenthal, who photographed U.S. Marines raising the American flag on Iwo Jima.
JIM HYSONG

and Gela landing beaches was the pinnacle of the trip. Memories and emotions, buried deep for 70 years, resurfaced. One of the organizers, Ornella Laneri, accompanied Phil to the Museum of the Catania Landings. "Walking alone, he stopped angrily in front of the reproduction of Hitler. He was indifferent to the (faux) debris in the displays because many of his comrades had died under the real rubble. He walked away for two minutes. Offstage in a corner he began a commentary, enunciating the names of his fellow Rangers who fell in Sicily. For the first time I realized that the island was wounded."

LEFT TOP Ranger Warren "Bing" Evans, top kick of E Company, lights up with a Commando instructor during a training break at the Commando Training Center in Achnacarry, Scotland, July 1942
PHIL STERN

LEFT Nearly 50 years later Commando Niall Thomson and Evans reenact the same scene from 1942 on the steps of the Commando Memorial Bridge, April 27, 1991. In the background are Alan Swanson, Mile Kness, Ray Rodriquez, Dave Frunder and Randall Harris.
PHIL STERN

Phil Stern
AND BING EVANS
ON PATROL.

READY
TO
KICK
SOME
PAVARAZIS'S
BUTTS!

PAVARAZIS
LET'M GET A
LITTLE
CLOSER ..
CLOSER ..

Bill Frake 2004

LEFT After a 50-year silence and some coaxing from a friend, Bing Evans began talking about his traumatic experiences in a German P.O.W. camp. He even wrote a book about it, entitled *Heroes Cry Too*. In this photograph, he is seen in Scotland on the Commando training grounds, accepting an award for Best Ranger in 1942.

PHIL STERN. ILLUSTRATION BY WILLIAM FRAKE

ABOVE In celebration of his 95th birthday on September 3, 2014, Phil donated 95 of his photographs to the West Los Angeles Veterans Home. During the event he was surprised with an official induction into the Ranger Hall of Fame. A few tears were seen rolling down the cheeks of the tough-as-nails Ranger. Here he is photographed with his cardboard cutout twin listening to the announcement of his induction into the Ranger Hall of Fame.

JOSEPH BONILLA

NEXT PAGE July 2013, Phil poses in front of the Gallery Credito in Catania, Sicily, for an exhibition of his photographs celebrating the 70th anniversary of the invasion. In September 2017, the Allied Landings in Sicily Museum opened the Phil Stern Pavilion, a permanent wing displaying his photographs through to 2032.

PETER STERN

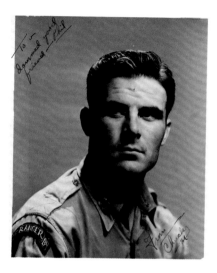 

ABOVE LEFT Chuck Shunstrom. The Boston native fought valiantly in all the major engagements of the Mediterranean Theater including Arzew, El Guettar, Sicily and Anzio. He was one of 50 Rangers to participate in the Dieppe Raid. Succumbing to the demons of war, in 1972 Shunstrom died alone in the aisle of a Buffalo, New York, convenience store. With help from his sister and Ranger friends, years later his ashes were interred at Arlington National Cemetery.
PHIL STERN

ABOVE RIGHT Back in the states after the disaster at Anzio, Colonel Darby took leave to visit his family in Ft. Smith Arkansas. This photo was taken during his visit. He was then appointed as a section chief of the General Staff's War Plans Division at the Pentagon, serving eleven months before returning to Italy. On April 30, 1945, a piece of German shrapnel pierced his heart, killing him instantly. Darby was posthumously promoted to brigadier general on May 15, 1945.
MITCHELL PHOTOGRAPHY FT SMITH, ARKANSAS

In early 2014, Phil decided it was time to move into the Veterans Home in West Los Angeles. A spry 94-year-old, he brought his scanners, computer and cameras, continuing to print photographs, signing and passing them out to residents and staff. After years of red tape, he was finally able to donate 100 of his prints to the newly built Cal Vet Home. Previously barren white walls are now adorned with images of the Rangers, Hollywood celebrities, jazz musicians and President Kennedy.

His 95th birthday was celebrated with 500 of his closest friends, family, admirers, fellow veterans and photographers. A 60-minute documentary of his time in Sicily was screened. TV reporters and local politicians stopped by. Fans waited in line for autographs and a chance to get their picture taken with the Snapdragon. The best surprise was saved for last. Phil was inducted into the prestigious Ranger Hall of Fame. He was bestowed this rare honor "for his

PHIL STERN. SICILY 1943
11.07 – 08.09.2013
GALLERIA CREDITO SICILIANO. ACIREALE
PHIL STERN. SICILY 1943
11.07 – 08.09.2013
GALLERIA CREDITO SICILIANO. ACIREALE
SU PRENOTAZIONE
INGRESSO LIBERO

service as an original member of the 1st Ranger Battalion and for his lasting contribution to the photographic history of the Rangers in the European Theater during World War II." A tear could be seen running down the rough 'n tough Ranger's face.

A poignant letter from Colonel Darby's nephews Darby and Presson Watkins and niece Sylvia Watkins Ryan was read aloud:

> *Few people realize that one of your greatest accomplishments was giving the American people black and white images of hope during those nerve-wracking early years of World War II. Darby's Rangers and other specialized military formations were some of the very first Americans to actively engage the Axis powers in combat.*

Phil "Snapdragon" Stern passed away on December 13, 2014. He was 95 years old.

You know, you'll never have a greater outfit

than the Rangers. What fighters and what buddies.

I'm proud to say I was one of them and I'm proud to say

that I was there.

Even in Eternity Phil Stern will Rule. Phil Stern passed away on December 13, 2014.
ILLUSTRATION BY BILL FRAKE

INDEX